C000218023

IMAGES
of Sport

NORWICH CITY
FOOTBALL CLUB

NORWICH CITY
FOOTBALL CLUB

F.A. CUP (FIRST ROUND PROPER)

SATURDAY, 15th NOVEMBER, 1958

Norwich City v. Ilford

PRICE **4d.** EACH

IMAGES
of Sport

NORWICH CITY
FOOTBALL CLUB

Compiled by
Gary Enderby

TEMPUS

First published 2001
Copyright © Gary Enderby, 2001

Tempus Publishing Limited
The Mill, Brimscombe Port,
Stroud, Gloucestershire, GL5 2QG

ISBN 0 7524 2266 9

Typesetting and origination by
Tempus Publishing Limited
Printed in Great Britain by
Midway Colour Print, Wiltshire

Also available from Tempus Publishing:

Contents

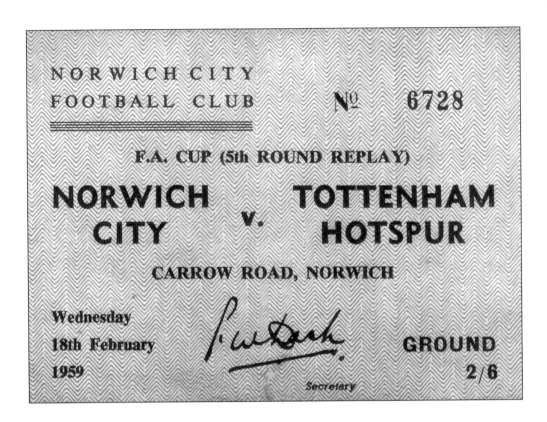

NORWICH CITY
FOOTBALL CLUB   No 6728

F.A. CUP (5th ROUND REPLAY)

NORWICH   TOTTENHAM
CITY   v.   HOTSPUR

CARROW ROAD, NORWICH

Wednesday
18th February   GROUND
1959   2/6

Secretary

Acknowledgements

Firstly, I would like to thank James Howarth of Tempus Publishing for giving me the initial opportunity to add Norwich City to their excellent images of sport series.

Thanks also to Mike Davage, the Norwich City historian, who gave me his permission to refer to his own works on Norwich City, including *Glorious Canaries and Canary Citizens*, which has helped a great deal with player information. Thanks also to Norwich City Football Club for use of club information. I would also like to thank friends and fellow City supporters – Ben Gray, Steve Denmark, Tony and Margaret Colman and John Keymer – who kindly lent me treasured items of City memorabilia, and to ex-Norwich City player Bill Punton, who most kindly wrote the foreword for this book.

Finally, thanks to Eastern Counties Newspapers, for allowing me to reproduce many of their photographs and newspaper headlines.

Gary Enderby

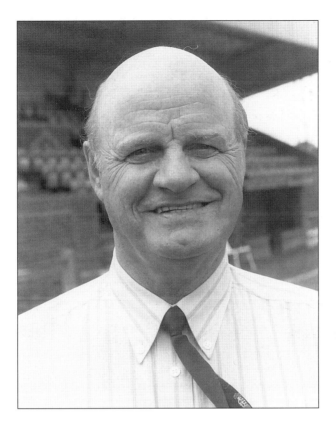

Foreword
by Bill Punton

I first heard of Norwich City when I was doing my national service at Catterick camp. I was playing for Newcastle United at the time and they arranged for me to be stationed there so I would be able to play for them every Saturday. Whilst playing with the British Army team I met a lad called Billy Coxon, who was in the team and was also playing for Norwich City. He gave me a glowing account of both the football club and the city itself – what a lovely place to live, being near beaches and broads.

I should have joined Norwich City from Newcastle along with Jimmy Hill, but Southend made a higher offer for me so I ended up there. A season later, however, I followed Errol Crossan from Southend to Norwich. Archie Macaulay was the City manager at the time, and wanted Crossan and myself at the same time, but Southend wouldn't let me go until the end of the season.

When I arrived at City I was very impressed, not just by the club, but by Norwich itself. It was just after the 1959 cup run and the whole city was bubbling, I couldn't believe the crowds we got at the games – there were often 20,000-30,000 and even more for some night games. In those days there was never any trouble and no segregation of supporters – they were all together and singing, not chanting.

Norwich was a real family club. The team spirit was first class and players used to socialise together, going out to meet the supporters at carnivals, beauty contests, fetes, etc. Often we went to villages to play the locals at cricket, darts, golf, snooker, tennis or bowls. At away matches, Ron Ashman used to collect the complimentary tickets (we used to get two each) and go outside the ground and give them to the travelling City supporters.

Training in those days was very hard. I dreaded the pre-season eight-mile runs – which we had every morning – the two hours of sprinting, the weights and running up and down hills at Mousehold Heath under the watchful eyes of the City trainers. I always did my road running in my army boots, so I never suffered from blisters like a lot of the players. By the start of the season we were all very fit and raring to go.

The boots and balls we used were so much heavier and it used to take us weeks to break our boots in. The leather ball, which absorbed the rain, sometimes weighed about four or five pounds – I've seen lots of players knocked out with it; I couldn't see David Beckham swerve his free kicks with that ball! On wet days it was all we could do to take corner kicks. I used to toe-end them like rugby players to get the ball into the goalmouth; Gerry Mannion was the only player to get corners to the far post – but then he had size twelve boots!

There were some great players at Norwich then: Barry Butler was the best centre-half in England in my opinion, but he only got selected twice for the FA team and didn't get a cap. It was the saddest day of my life when he was killed in a car crash, as we were great friends. Ron Davies was a superb centre forward – he was a regular in the Welsh team and the best striker Norwich City ever had in my own opinion. Matt Crowe was a great midfield player, in the class of Ian Crook or Martin Peters when they played for Norwich.

Whilst at Norwich I played under five managers: Archie Macaulay, Willie Reid, George Swindin, Ron Ashman and Lol Morgan, and they were all different in their approach to the game. Archie Macaulay was, however, head and shoulders above the rest both in tactics and spotting weaknesses in the opposing teams. Many times we would come in at half-time 1-0 down and he would change our formation, even switching Crossan and myself to opposite wings and tell us to attack the full-backs on the inside, as he had spotted they could only tackle with the one foot. The result of such leadership was often that we would come in at the end of such matches having won 3-1 or 4-1 and overrun the opposition.

It was a sad day for me when Lol Morgan sold me to Sheffield United, who were in the First Division. I refused to move house as I had so many friends in Norfolk; I loved the place, and had made up my mind to settle there. Norwich City granted me permission to train with them and I travelled to all the Sheffield games. Although I only trained under him, Ron Saunders impressed me with the way he went about the job of manager. The training was so hard I decided to take an afternoon off once and the next day he had me in his office and telephoned John Harris, the Sheffield United manager, to report me. He said he wanted me to be there whilst he did it and I respected him for doing that. I couldn't take the hard training at thirty-three, so I got permission to train mornings only. Ron Saunders, when he was at City, had the fittest team in the League and turned mediocre players into some of the most useful in the country.

Whilst at Newcastle United, I thought that their supporters were the most knowledgeable about football in the country, but City fans come a close second, supporting their club through good and bad times. They really deserve Premiership football and, hopefully, in the not-too-distant future they will achieve just that.

Bill Punton
June 2001

One

Southern League Days

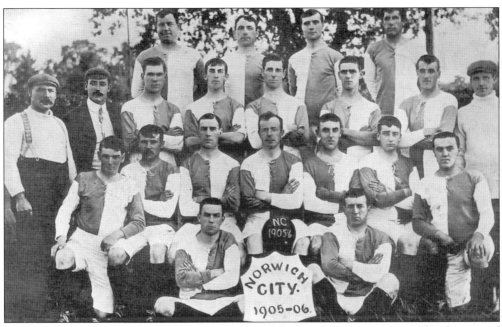

From 1902 to 1905, Norwich City played in the Norfolk & Suffolk League. In 1905/06 they joined the Southern League and this photograph is from that first season as a professional outfit. The team are wearing the club colours of blue and white halves. City's first match in the Southern League was an away trip to Plymouth, which they lost 2-0. City finally finished seventh and were knocked out in the second round of the FA Cup by Second Division Manchester United. From left to right, back row: A. Archer, J. McEwen (captain), W. Bushell, Warnes. Third row: C. Miles (trainer), J. Bowman (manager), B. Childs, B. Cummings, C. Williams, F. Rose, F. Bemment, H. McQueen (assistant trainer). Second row: R. Muir, S. Graham, F. Wilkinson, D. Ronaldson, D. Ross, H. Brindley, W. Linward. Front row: H. Vigar, A. Livingstone.

James McEwen was City's first professional captain and the only ever-present player in the club's first season of Southern League football, also playing in all four FA Cup matches. 'Punch', as he was known, was born in Liverpool and played at left-back for City from 1905 to 1908, making a total of 121 appearances in league and cup competition.

Davie Ross was top scorer for City in their first two seasons of Southern League football with 17 league goals in 1905/06 and 19 in the 1906/07 season from just the first 24 league games. Ross was transferred in February 1907 to First Division Manchester City for a Southern League record fee of £650. He had scored 49 goals for City in just 71 appearances and, understandably, the Norwich supporters were upset when he was sold. Both McEwen and Ross had previously played for Bury in the First Division of the Football League.

Fred Thompson was a goalkeeper who took over from Charles Williams for the 1906/07 season, becoming an ever-present in all Southern League and FA Cup matches during that campaign. He had previously kept goal for FA Cup winners Bury in 1899/1900, when they defeated Southampton 4-0 in the final. He made a total of 67 league and cup appearances for Norwich City.

Archie Livingstone was a right-half and one of just eleven players to have played in over 100 Southern League games for City. He had helped Burnley win the Second Division in 1897/98 and joined Norwich at the beginning of the 1905/06 season, making his debut at home to Watford in September. He made a total of 134 league and cup appearances (including United League matches), scoring twice.

WIlliam Bushell was a half-back and made his debut in City's first Southern League match at Plymouth, missing just two matches in that first season. He made a total of 132 Southern League appearances (including 51 as captain) and 154 in all competitions (including United League and FA Cup games), scoring 4 times between 1905 and 1910.

William Wood, known as 'Billy', was an inside forward. He joined City from Fulham, but had previously won two FA Cup winners' medals with First Division Bury in 1899/1900 and in 1902/03 (the 6-0 defeat of Derby County), scoring once in both games. He joined Norwich in 1906, making his home debut against Portsmouth in March. He finished as second highest top scorer in Southern League matches behind Davie Ross in 1906/07, but moved on in 1907, joining Southern League rivals Leyton. He totalled 57 league and cup appearances for City, scoring 17 goals.

Glaswegian Duncan Ronaldson was a centre forward. Born in 1880, he made 89 Southern League appearances for City, scoring 15 goals – including City's first away goal in the Southern League at Reading in a 3-1 defeat. After leaving City for Brighton in May 1907, he rejoined City in 1909, playing for one more season, 1909/10. He made a total of 109 league and cup appearances, scoring 27 goals.

Percy Gooch, known as 'Put', was a centre forward who made his City debut against his home-town club, Lowestoft, in a FA Cup preliminary round match in September 1903, scoring a hat-trick in a 4-1 victory. City were a Norfolk & Suffolk League side at the time, and 'Put' made his professional debut at Brighton in April 1906 in his only appearance during City's first Southern League season, scoring in a 2-0 win. He then left the club, but returned in the 1909/10 season to score another 12 goals in a further 20 Southern League games before retiring at the end of the campaign to become the trainer for Lowestoft Town. He totalled 65 appearances in all competitions, scoring 36 goals.

John William Bowman was City's first professional manager, joining the club in April 1905. He had previously played for Burslem Port Vale, Stoke and Queens Park Rangers, and it was said of him that 'His practical and business-like qualities, combined with his straightforward manner, have gained for him the respect of all with whom he has come in contact'. Bowman made 8 appearances for City as a player, including one FA Cup game.

SOUTHERN LEAGUE, 1905-6.

	Matches Played.	Home. W. L. D. Gls.	Away. W. L. D. Gls.	Pts.
Fulham ...	34...10	0 7 (22— 6)...9	3 5 (22— 9)...50	
Southampton	34...13	2 2 (32—11)...6	6 5 (26—28)...45	
Portsmouth...	34...13	1 3 (39—11)...4	7 6 (22—24)...43	
Luton Town	34...13	2 2 (45—13)...4	8 5 (19 –27)...41	
T. Hotspur ...	34...13	2 2 (36—11)...3	9 5 (10 –18) ..39	
Plymouth Ar.	34...11	3 3 (32—13)...5	8 4 (20 - 20)...39	
Norwich City	34... 8	1 8 (30—12)...5	10 2 (16—26)...36	
Bristol Rovr's	34...11	5 1 (37—23)...4	9 4 (19—33)...35	
Brentford ...	34...11	3 3 (28—19)...3	10 4 (15—33)...35	
Reading	34... 9	1 7 (34—15)...3	12 2 (19—31).. 33	
Millwall	34... 9	4 4 (26—16)...2	8 7 (12—25)...33	
West Ham ...	34...12	3 2 (30— 9)...2	12 3 (12—30)...33	
Q. P. Rangers	34... 9	5 3 (39—14) ..3	10 4 (19 - 30)...31	
Watford	34... 7	4 6 (28—20)...1	12 4 (10—37)...26	
Swindon T.	34... 6	7 4 (21—23)...2	10 5 (10—29)...25	
Brighton	34... 8	4 5 (24—24)...1	14 2 (6—31)...25	
N. Brompton	34... 5	7 5 (10—20)...2	12 3 (10—42)...22	
Northampton	34... 5	8 4 (17—22)...3	13 1 (15—57)...21	

The Southern League table for City's first season, 1905/06, as shown in the following season's club handbook. City's final position of seventh was the best in their Southern League spell (eleven seasons from 1905 to 1915 and then one more season after the First World War). Meanwhile, over in the Football League in 1905/06, Liverpool were First Division Champions and Manchester United had won promotion from the Second Division.

City's side for their second season in the Southern League, 1906/07. The players are in blue and white halved shirts and are lined up as follows, from left to right, back row: C. Miles (trainer), A. Archer (vice-captain), P. McLarney, J.W. Cannon, F. Thompson, P. Gooch, A. Livingstone, F. Bemment, W. Bushell, H. McQueen (assistant trainer). Middle row: J. McEwen (captain), A. Birnie, J. Byrne, J.W. Bowman (manager), G. Lamberton, A. Liddell, D. Ross, H. Brindley. Front row: R. Muir, W. Wood, D. Ronaldson, J. Chalmers.

Norwich City FC, 1907/08. The players are now wearing their new colours of yellow shirts with green collars and cuffs (even at this early stage, reference was already being made to 'The Canaries'). From left to right, back row: Peter Roney, Fred Thompson. Third row: William Bushell, Albert Jones, Bobby Whiteman, Archie Livingstone, Gerry Newlands, Hugh McQueen (assistant trainer). Second row: Robert Muir, George Lamberton, James McEwen, Wally Smith, Tommy Allsopp. Front row: James Young, James Bauchop, Harry Hutchison.

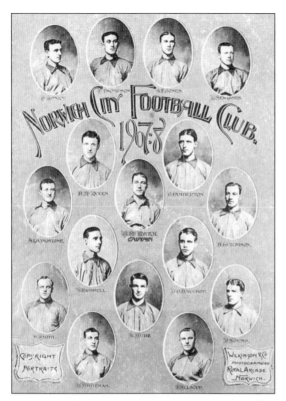

Norwich City player photographs, 1907/08. This was to be City's last season playing at Newmarket Road, before their move to The Nest. Their league form was mainly uneventful, and the biggest talking point of the season was City's first ever giant-killing act. They welcomed First Division Sheffield Wednesday, the 1907 FA Cup holders, in a first round tie and beat them 2-0. This was the last FA Cup match to be held at Newmarket Road as City lost 2-1 at Second Division Fulham in the second round.

The 1907/08 team and officials. From left to right, back row: A. Turner (assistant manager), T. Bury (director), F.A. Kent (clerk), A.E. Barham (director), M. Nattrass (director), W.T. Blyth (director). Third row: H. McQueen (trainer), G. Newlands, R. Whiteman, J. Youngs, H. Hutchison, A.T. Jones, F. Thompson, P. Roney, J.W. Howes (director and honorary secretary). Second row: T. Allsopp, G. Lamberton, J.R. Bauchop, R. Webster (vice-chairman), G.M. Chamberlin (director), J. Pyke (chairman), J. McEwen (captain), W. Bushell, A. Livingstone. Front row: F. Muir, W. Smith.

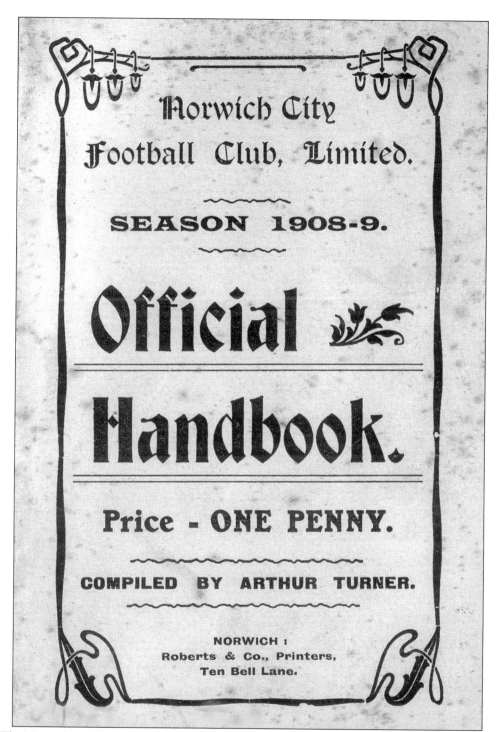

Norwich City Football Club, Limited.

SEASON 1908-9.

Official

Handbook.

Price - ONE PENNY.

COMPILED BY ARTHUR TURNER.

NORWICH :
Roberts & Co., Printers,
Ten Bell Lane.

The Norwich City handbook for the 1908/09 season, compiled by the assistant manager Arthur Turner. This was City's first season at The Nest, and Mr Turner noted in his introduction – 'The change of the ground should make for a larger support, and I hope the "Canaries" will thrive at their new home, "The Nest".'

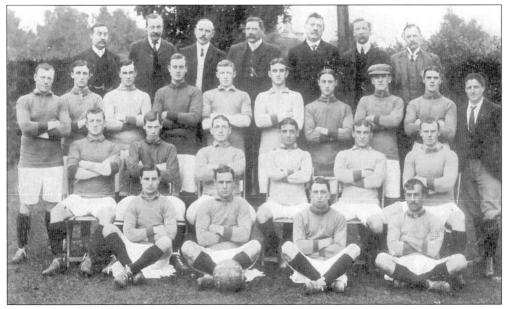

The 1908/09 team postcard. City enjoyed more FA Cup thrills during this season, with the giant-killing of First Division Liverpool at Anfield 3-2 to reach the third round for the first time. The next round, however, saw defeat away at another First Division club, Bristol City, 2-0. Bristol City went on to reach the final, but lost to Manchester United. In the league Norwich finished nineteenth – the club's lowest placing in their eleven seasons of Southern League football.

Peter Roney was a goalkeeper who played for the best part of the 1907/08 season, replacing Fred Thompson but missing several games through injury. He was the unfortunate 'keeper who conceded ten goals in City's record 10-2 defeat at the hands of Swindon Town at the beginning of the 1908/09 season. His career at Norwich ended the same season when he broke his collarbone in the match at Brentford on 9 April, but he later transferred to play for Bristol Rovers. He made a total of 69 appearances for City.

George Newlands, popularly known as 'Jerry', was a right-back who made his City debut at the beginning of the 1907/08 season, making 34 league appearances. He was the most consistent player in 1908/09, appearing in a further 35 league games and all 5 FA Cup encounters as City reached the third round for the first time. Newlands made a total of 111 appearances and scored one goal, at Plymouth in March 1909.

Thomas Allsopp was a forward who scored on his debut in the first match of the 1907/08 season, at home to Portsmouth on 2 September. He scored a total of 9 goals that season, including one against Sheffield Wednesday in the famous FA Cup win. He made 115 Southern League appearances for City (scoring 18 league goals) and accumulated an overall total of 132 appearances and 27 goals.

John Flanagan was an inside forward who made his debut against Reading on 22 February 1908. He scored just once in 10 appearances during that campaign, and managed to score only once more in 24 Southern League appearances in the following season. He totalled 43 games overall, scoring 4 times. He left City to join Fulham and later enjoyed a more prolific spell with First Division Woolwich Arsenal.

Cyril Dunning was a forward who made his debut against Ipswich Town on 5 April 1904 in a Norfolk & Suffolk League match (his one and only appearance in that competition). He rejoined City in June 1907, playing 5 times at the end of the 1907/08 season, scoring 3 times. He was the top league goalscorer for the club in 1908/09, hitting 15 in just 21 Southern League matches. He totalled 50 appearances overall, scoring 27 goals.

John Smith was a forward who joined City in May 1908, making his debut at the beginning of the 1908/09 season at Luton Town. He made all his City appearances in that season, and finished as top goalscorer with 24 in Southern League, United League and FA Cup matches. Smith's one and only FA Cup goal was the dramatic last-minute winner that saw off First Division Liverpool at Anfield in front of 32,000 fans (the highest crowd City played in front of as a Southern League team). He totalled 41 games and 24 goals for Norwich.

Robert Beale, a goalkeeper, made his debut for City on 14 November 1908 against Plymouth Argyle. He had tough competition from Peter Roney for the 'keeper's shirt for much of the season, but took over on a more regular basis when Roney broke his collarbone at Brentford towards the end of the 1908/09 season. Beale made 10 appearances in that inaugural campaign, but after Roney left the club was first choice goalkeeper for the next three seasons, making a total of 111 appearances (105 of these being in Southern League matches). He left City in May 1912 to join First Division Manchester United and made his debut on 2 September 1912 in the first match of the 1912/13 season against Woolwich Arsenal, a goalless draw. He went on to make a total of 112 appearances for United before retiring in 1921.

William Silor was a forward who made his debut on 2 September 1908 away at Luton in the first game of the 1908/09 season. He had just one season with City, making 27 appearances and scoring 7 times in Southern League matches. He left the club in May 1909 to join Southern League rivals West Ham United. He played a total of 36 games for City, scoring 11 goals (including United League matches).

Hugh McQueen was City's trainer and 'A Scot – no possible doubt about it' according to the notes in the 1908/09 handbook. Hugh had played for many clubs, but enjoyed most success with Liverpool, Derby County and Queens Park Rangers. He played under John Bowman at QPR and it was Bowman that brought him to Norwich as trainer after he took over as manager. He stayed with the club as trainer until 1910, and made one playing appearance in a United League match on 15 March 1909 at Rotherham Town, but ended up on the losing side in a 6-1 defeat.

Arthur Turner, City's assistant manager, played an important part in the formation of the club and brought many players to Norwich. The 1908/09 handbook said 'Mr Turner has done much more than his share of work in connection with Norwich City. Quiet and unassuming, he has gained the confidence of the players and officials of the club, and is admirably fitted for his office. He has been remarkably successful in obtaining the services of many young players, many of whom have been, and will be, of great use to the club.'

Norwich City FC, 1912/13. City struggled in the league in this season, finishing eighteenth with their lowest points haul for a Southern League campaign. In the FA Cup they played five matches, although only reached the second round. An abandoned game with Second Division Leicester Fosse was finally won at Leicester 4-1, and three matches with Southern League rivals Bristol Rovers saw them eventually go down 1-0 in the second replay at Stamford Bridge.

Postcard for the Brighton & Hove Albion *v.* Norwich City match at Hove on 2 November 1912. City had suffered defeats in their previous four away matches, but managed a 2-2 draw at Brighton, William Ingham and William Hughes scoring for City. The crowd was recorded as 5,000.

Two
The Third Division
and Promotion

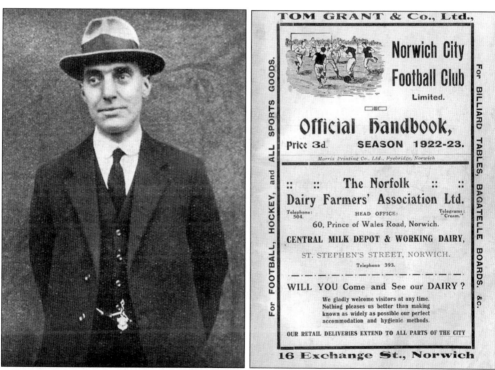

Left: Manager Albert Arthur Gosnell replaced Charles O'Hagen, City's first Football League manager who had been appointed in July 1920. Gosnell was appointed during the second half of City's inaugural League season, 1920/21. *Right:* The 1922/23 handbook. City finished eighteenth at the end of this campaign, their third in the Third Division (South), and reached the first round of the FA Cup by beating Ilford. It was the first FA Cup meeting between the two sides and City won 5-1. Their second meeting many years later was, of course, to have far more significance.

Irish born William O'Hagan was a goalkeeper. He had two international caps for Ireland against England and Wales. He made his City debut against Exeter City on 11 March 1922, replacing Herbert Skermer, and went on to make a total of 57 League and cup appearances.

James Hodge was a full-back who played for Manchester United until 1914/15, when he was dropped to make way for his younger brother, John. After serving in the war, he was sold to Millwall Athletic for £1,500 and joined Norwich in January 1922, making his City debut against Millwall on 23 February 1922. He made a total of 55 League and cup appearances, scoring one goal, against Newport County in March 1923. He left in September of the same year to join Southend United.

Philip Hope was a full-back who made his City debut in the club's last Southern League season on 7 February 1920 at home to Southend United. He made 118 appearances for Norwich, scoring his one and only goal for the club in his penultimate game for City at home to Queens Park Rangers on 21 April 1924. One month later, he joined First Division Blackburn Rovers.

Samuel William Austin, an outside-right, started his career as a goalkeeper for his local side, Arnold United, and also played for Arnold St Mary's before coming to Norwich in October 1920. He made his debut on 23 October 1920 at Bristol Rovers in City's first season as a Football League side. He was the top goalscorer in 1921/22 with 12 League and cup goals. Austin played a total of 164 matches for City, scoring 39 times before moving to First Division Manchester City in May 1924.

Robert Dennison, an inside forward, was a team-mate of Austin at Arnold St Mary's before coming to Norwich. He made his debut on 11 September 1920 against Crystal Palace. City had started their Football League campaign without scoring in their first five home games until Dennison's goal against Bristol Rovers on 30 October in a 1-1 draw. Having become the first League goalscorer on home turf for Norwich, he became the first to score a hat-trick when he grabbed all the goals in a 3-2 home win over Millwall on 14 April 1923. He made 126 appearances and scored 38 goals for City before leaving in 1924 for Brighton. Dennison later joined Austin at Manchester City in May 1925.

George Martin, a centre-half, was familiar to everyone as 'Pompey' – he had previously played for Sunderland and Portsmouth before joining City in July 1913. He made his Norwich debut on 13 September 1913 in a Southern League match at Southend United. After the war, he continued to play a big part in the City side and made a total of 337 appearances for Norwich, scoring once in a 6-3 win over Bournemouth in 1924. He left the club in 1927, playing until the end of the 1926/27 season.

James Hannah was a centre forward and half-back. Born in Sheringham, Hannah made a total of 427 appearances for Norwich City, scoring 21 goals. He made his City debut on 13 January 1921 at Newport County in his only outing of the 1920/21 season, but his City first-team career extended over fifteen seasons until the club's Second Division days in 1934/35. He was still scoring for City reserves in 1937 and was the club's assistant trainer in 1945/46.

James Stoakes was an outside-left who joined City in April 1921 and made his debut on 8 September 1921 at home to Plymouth Argyle. He was an ever-present in the 1922/23 side, playing in all 46 League and FA Cup games, and went on to make a total of 150 appearances for City, scoring 6 goals.

Benjamin George Smith was a full-back. Born in Norwich, 'Bennie' joined City in April 1915, but had to wait another four years to make his debut, due to the outbreak of the First World War. His debut finally came on the opening day of the 1919/20 season at home to Newport County in a Southern League match on 30 August and was part of a 4-1 victory. He is one of only three players who played in the FA Cup for City as both a Southern League and Football League player and he made a total of 110 appearances (including Southern League and Football League matches).

Jobling. Hannah, Lochhead, Scott. Crompton, Wharton, Brain, Wallbanks, Wren, Thompson, Robinson,
Young, Hunt, Burditt, Smith, Jordan, Ogle, Williamson, Williams, Murphy, Blakemore, Hawes,
(Trainer) McGregor, Taylor, Brown, Pearson, Bell, Slack, Hall. (Asst. Trainer)

NORWICH CITY FOOTBALL TEAM. 1931—1932.

The 1931/32 Norwich City team wearing yellow and green halved shirts. City finished tenth in the Third Division (South), enjoying high-scoring home wins over Thames (7-0), Bristol Rovers (6-0) and Coventry City (6-2). They did, however, suffer a 7-1 defeat at Luton Town – although overall it was all a great improvement on the previous season's performances, which had left the club bottom of the table.

The Norwich City *v.* Bristol Rovers souvenir programme for the last match of the 1933/34 season on Saturday 5 May 1934. City were Third Division champions and duly promoted to the Second Division for the first time. A crowd of 13,899 witnessed a goalless draw, but City were already clear at the top of the table by 7 points and replaced Millwall in the Second Division for 1934/35.

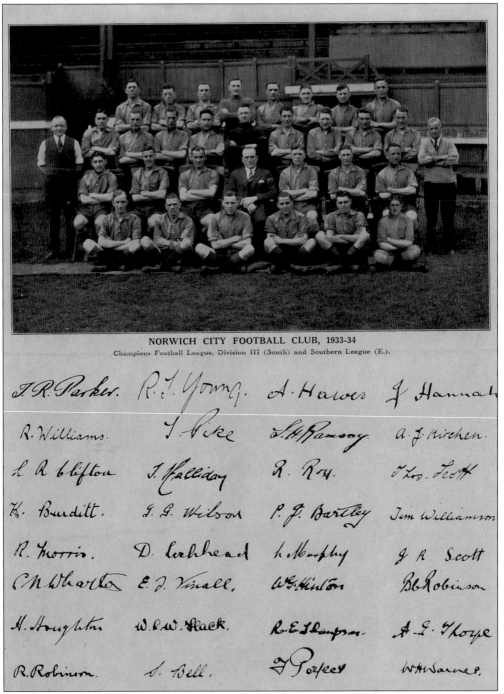

NORWICH CITY FOOTBALL CLUB, 1933-34

Champions Football League, Division III (South) and Southern League (E.).

(Autographed team sheet with signatures:)

T. R. Parker.   R. J. Young.   A. Hawes   J. Hannah

R. Williams.   T. Pike   J. H. Ramsay   A. J. Kirchen.

L. R. Clifton   J. Halliday   R. Roy.   Jno. Scott

H. Burditt.   J. G. Wilson   P. J. Bartley   Jim Williamson

R. Morris.   D. Lochhead   L. Murphy   J. R. Scott

C. M. Wharton   E. J. Vinall.   W. G. Hinton   B. B. Robinson

H. Houghton   W. R. W. Slack.   R. E. Sampson.   A. G. Thorpe

R. Robinson.   S. Bell.   J. Porfect   W. H. Warnes.

An autographed team sheet from the 1933/34 season. City had previously been champions of the Norfolk & Suffolk League in 1904/05, and the winning of the Third Division (South) was their first major honour after fourteen seasons in the League.

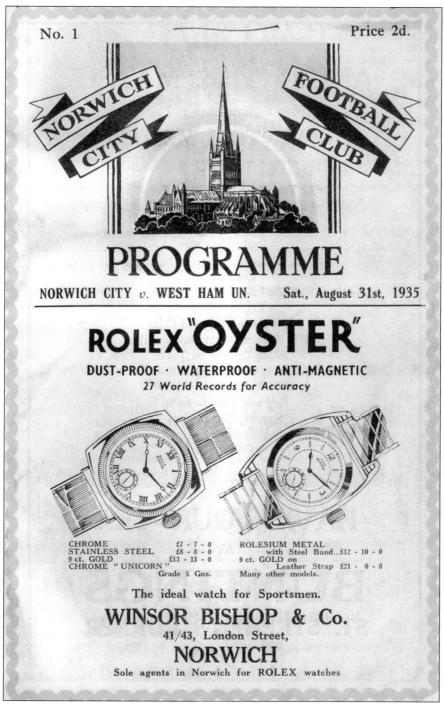

The very first match at City's new ground at Carrow Road was against West Ham United for a Second Division game on Saturday 31 August 1935. The crowd of 29,779 was the biggest up to that time to watch Norwich on home soil and they saw a thrilling 4-3 win for City. Captain Doug Lochhead scored the first goal for Norwich at Carrow Road, with Billy Warnes and Jack Vinall (2) also finding the net on the day.

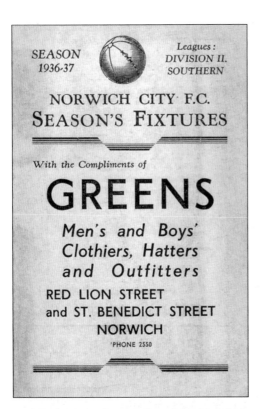

The fixture card for the 1936/37 season. City had reached the fifth round of the FA Cup for the first time in 1934/35, knocking out First Division Leeds United 2-1 away before losing 0-1 at home to Sheffield Wednesday before a record crowd at The Nest of 25,037. In the following season they finished eleventh in the Second Division, with Jack Vinall scoring 24 League goals.

Norwich finished seventeenth in the Second Division in 1936/37, but knocked First Division Liverpool out of the FA Cup 3-0 at home before going down to Bolton Wanderers, another First Division side, 2-1 at home after holding them to a 1-1 draw at Bolton.

The souvenir programme for the visit of George VI to Carrow Road for the Second Division game with Millwall on Saturday 29 October 1938. City lost the game 2-0 in front of 21,593 spectators.

NORWICH CITY
FOOTBALL CLUB

OFFICIAL HANDBOOK AND DIARY 1939·40

Caley
of NORWICH

MANUFACTURERS
of GOOD
CHOCOLATES

OBTAINABLE FROM ALL ATTENDANTS
ON THE GROUND

PRICE 3d.

The Norwich City handbook for the 1939/40 season. Norwich had been relegated at the end of the previous season back down to the Third Division (South) after just five seasons in the Second, but would have to wait another seven years before they could even begin to regain their place back in the higher division. City played just three matches of the 1939/40 season – losing 2-1 at home to Cardiff, winning 2-1 at Bristol City and drawing 1-1 at Ipswich – when war was declared the day after the lattermost result. Although the League programme was suspended, there were still regional league matches played throughout the war years.

John Church, an outside right or left, joined City in 1936 after playing as an amateur for Lowestoft Town. He made his Norwich debut as an eighteen-year-old at Barnsley on 23 April 1938 in a goalless draw. He made just 13 League appearances for City before the Second World War interrupted his career, but did also play in all of the three matches of 1939/40 (which do not count in League career records). He next played in the 1945/46 Third Division regional cup competition, scoring four goals in a 6-1 home win over Crystal Palace. His final League appearance for City was on 29 April 1950 at home to Southend United, as he joined Colchester United in the summer. He made a total of 114 appearances for City, scoring 16 goals.

Harry Dukes, a goalkeeper, was born in Portsmouth but moved to Suffolk and played for several local clubs, including Ipswich Town. Signed for Norwich in August 1934, he made his debut against Plymouth Argyle at home on 15 September 1934 in a 3-0 win. His surname in City handbooks and records is actually 'Duke' – due to a cartoon depicting Harry with that name which, despite his protests, stuck. He made 124 appearances for City, which included keeping goal in the last match at The Nest and the first at Carrow Road. He was also custodian in the three matches of the abortive 1939/40 season, and returned to play for City in 1946/47, making 16 more appearances before finally leaving the club in 1947.

William Isaac Furness was an inside or outside-left. He played for Leeds United for eight seasons and appeared for England in 1933 against Italy in Rome. He broke his collarbone playing for Leeds United against Norwich in a FA Cup tie in 1935, but in 1937 joined Norwich for a fee of £2,750. Furness made his City debut at the beginning of the 1937/38 season against Southampton, scoring twice in a 4-3 home victory on 28 August. He made the most appearances of any Norwich player in that season and scored 11 goals, and he played in all of City's 43 games the following season (although the 7 goals he scored couldn't save City from relegation). He played for one more season after the war, making a total of 96 League and cup appearances and scoring 21 goals. He later returned to the club as a trainer and physiotherapist.

Frank Manders, an outside-left or inside forward, joined City from Crystal Palace in 1935, making his debut at home against Burnley on 26 October 1935. He scored 9 times in his first season, but was top scorer in 1936/37 with 17 and again in 1938/39 with just 8 as City were relegated. He made a total of 137 appearances for Norwich City, scoring 43 goals.

Michael Harry Proctor was a half-back who could play in any position, but made his Norwich City debut wearing the number 6 shirt against Sheffield United at home on 3 November 1934. He played in 100 friendly games for the club during the war years and returned to playing League football after the war, before becoming City's coach and trainer until August 1956. He made 116 appearances for Norwich, scoring 3 goals.

Tom Smalley, a left-half, joined City from Wolverhampton Wanderers in August 1938, having also played for England against Wales in 1937. Tom made his City debut in the relegation season, on 27 August 1938 at home to Bradford Park Avenue, appearing in all of the club's 43 matches that season. He made no further appearances for City, apart from the three games of the expunged 1939/40 campaign. He scored one goal, at home to Swansea, on 15 October 1938.

Maurice Tobin, a left-back, was secured from a junior side in his birthplace of Longriggend in Airdrie in 1938. He had to wait until 7 September 1946, however, to make his City debut, eventually playing at Ipswich. He made his final appearance against Walsall on 13 September 1950. In all, Tobin made 105 appearances for City before taking on a role with the coaching staff.

Harry Ware, a centre forward, had previously been with Stoke City, Newcastle United and Sheffield Wednesday before joining City in 1937. He made his Norwich debut on 13 November 1937 at home to Tottenham Hotspur and scored a goal in a 2-1 win. He made 45 appearances for the Canaries, scoring 14 goals.

Ernest Coleman, an inside-right who was known as 'Tim', had previously played for Halifax Town, Grimsby Town, Arsenal and Middlesbrough before joining City in February 1937. He made his debut at West Ham United on 13 February 1937 and scored 6 goals in just 14 games that season. He went on to become top scorer in the following season, 1937/38, with 16. Coleman was dealt a blow in the opening game of the 1938/39 season, when he was injured in the first few minutes of the game at home to Bradford Park Avenue and didn't play again until March. He made a total of 64 appearances for City, scoring 26 goals.

During the war years, City played in a regional league and friendly matches. This is a single sheet programme from a friendly v. Southend United on 16 September 1939. The game ended 6-2 in Southend's favour.

This match at Southend on 17 February 1940 was a regional league fixture and attracted just 500 spectators. The game ended as a 3-0 win for Southend.

Les Maskell, a centre forward, was born in Cowes on the Isle of Wight in 1918. Les had played for and won medals with the Hampshire school side before moving to Norwich as a sixteen-year-old in 1933. He joined the Norwich City groundstaff and went on to play for the Norwich City 'A' team before signing as a professional in 1936. He made his Football League debut at Plymouth Argyle on 5 February 1938 and made just 7 appearances for the club, scoring twice. During the war he netted a further 224 goals in friendly games, war league, 'A' and reserve team matches, and after the war he played for local clubs Lowestoft and Diss Town.

Norwich City sent a team to neighbouring Diss on Tuesday 5 April 1949 to mark the Norfolk & Suffolk League club's jubilee celebrations. A crowd of 2,000 packed into the Roydon Road ground to watch a Norwich City XI play a Diss XI – which included Alec Thurlow, the Manchester City goalkeeper, who came from Diss. The following season, Les Maskell joined Diss as their player-coach.

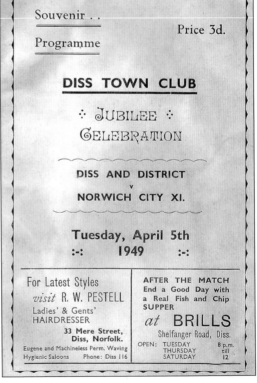

Souvenir . .

Programme

Price 3d.

DISS TOWN CLUB

⁘ JUBILEE ⁘
CELEBRATION

DISS AND DISTRICT
v
NORWICH CITY XI.

Tuesday, April 5th
:-: 1949 :-:

For Latest Styles	AFTER THE MATCH
visit R. W. PESTELL	End a Good Day with a Real Fish and Chip SUPPER
Ladies' & Gents' HAIRDRESSER	*at* BRILLS
33 Mere Street, Diss, Norfolk.	Shelfanger Road, Diss.
Eugene and Machineless Perm. Waving	OPEN: TUESDAY 8 p.m. THURSDAY till
Hygienic Saloons Phone: Diss 116	SATURDAY 12

42

There was no Football League action in 1945/46, but the FA Cup did commence again. City played one tie against Brighton in the third round over two legs, losing 2-1 at home and 4-1 away. This programme is from the first leg at Carrow Road on 5 January 1946.

NORWICH CITY

Football Club

●

PROGRAMME
for

Saturday, Jan. 5th

PRICE TWOPENCE

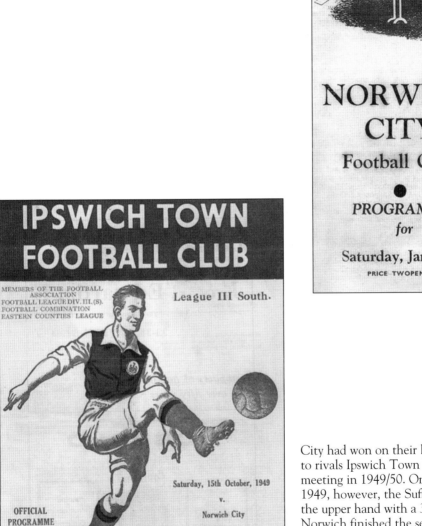

IPSWICH TOWN FOOTBALL CLUB

MEMBERS OF THE FOOTBALL
ASSOCIATION
FOOTBALL LEAGUE DIV. III. (S).
FOOTBALL COMBINATION
EASTERN COUNTIES LEAGUE

League III South.

OFFICIAL
PROGRAMME
3d.

Saturday, 15th October, 1949

v.

Norwich City

Kick-off 3.0 p.m.

EAST ANGLIAN DAILY TIMES CO. LTD.
PRINTERS
13, CARR STREET, IPSWICH.   PHONE 3204.

City had won on their last two visits to rivals Ipswich Town before this meeting in 1949/50. On 15 October 1949, however, the Suffolk rivals got the upper hand with a 3-0 win. Norwich finished the season eleventh in the Third Division (South), whilst Ipswich were seventeenth. City narrowly missed out on promotion the following season, finishing second behind champions Nottingham Forest, and got back to winning ways at Portman Road with a 1-0 victory.

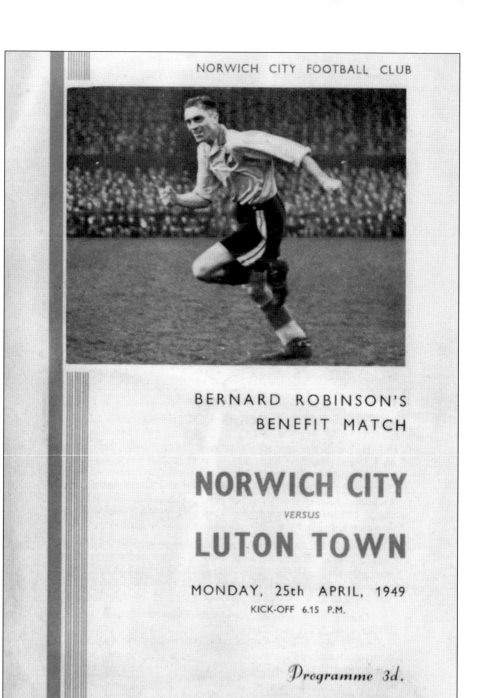

BERNARD ROBINSON'S
BENEFIT MATCH

NORWICH CITY

VERSUS

LUTON TOWN

MONDAY, 25th APRIL, 1949

KICK-OFF 6.15 P.M.

Programme 3d.

The testimonial programme for Bernard Cecil Robinson. Second Division Luton Town were the opponents on 25 April 1949 and they beat City 2-1. Robinson, a right half-back, played for Kings Lynn as a amateur and signed for City in December 1931. He was said to be one of the longest throwers of a ball in the game, and he made his debut for City on 2 April 1932 at Exeter City. He became a regular member of the side up until the war and played 160 games during the war years. He carried on with City in the Third Division (South) in 1946 and played for them until 1949, making a total of 380 appearances and scoring 14 goals.

NORWICH CITY FOOTBALL CLUB LIMITED

F.A. CUP THIRD ROUND PROPER
(REPLAY)

NORWICH CITY

v.

PORTSMOUTH

THURSDAY, 12th JANUARY, 1950
CARROW ROAD - NORWICH

Kick-off 2 p.m.

Norwich reached the third round of the FA Cup in 1949/50 and met Portsmouth, the current First Division champions. City came away with a very creditable 1-1 draw. The replay at Carrow Road, played on 12 January 1950 in front of a crowd of 43,129, saw them lose 2-0. Portsmouth went on to become League champions yet again that season.

Norwich City have featured on several cigarette cards. Clockwise: J. Gallaher card showing William Bushell, 1909/10; Ogdens card from the AFC nicknames set of 1933, depicting the Norwich canary; John Player card from 1928/29 showing Beccles-born goalkeeper Charles Dennington; Carreras card showing Edward Vinall, 1936; Ardath Cork card of William Warnes, 1934; Churchman card of Ernest Coleman, 1938.

Three
The 1950s and the Cup Run

Norwich City, 1951/52. In the previous season, City had at last challenged again for promotion, but had finally finished as runners-up behind Nottingham Forest. They also reached the fifth round of the FA Cup, losing 3-1 at Sunderland. City finished third in 1951/52, just 5 points behind champions Plymouth Argyle.

Ken Nethercott, a goalkeeper, made his City debut on 27 September 1947 in a Third Division (South) match at Northampton. He made a total of 416 appearances for the Canaries, including games in the famous 1959 FA Cup run – where he unfortunately dislocated his shoulder in the quarter-final match at Sheffield United, but carried on playing with his right arm out of action, earning his side a 1-1 draw and a reply at Carrow Road (which he would miss out on). In fact, that game against the Blades was to be his last for the club.

John Duffy, a right-back, made his debut for City on 31 December 1949 in a Third Division (South) match at home to Brighton. He made a total of 87 appearances before leaving the club for Yarmouth Town in 1954.

Bill Lewis, a left-back, made his City debut on 12 November 1949 at Watford and made 256 appearances for the club, scoring just one goal. He played his final game for the Canaries in 1955. Lewis later became the club coach and reserve team trainer.

Ron Ashman, a left half, played for City in a wartime friendly in 1944 and made his Norwich peacetime debut on 4 October 1947 at home to Aldershot. He became City's acting manager in December 1962 and manager from December 1963 until June 1966. Ashman made a total of 662 appearances for City – putting him second in the all-time appearance chart for the Canaries – scoring 56 goals and playing in ten of the eleven FA Cup matches in 1959. He was awarded an FA twenty-year service statuette and is one of the greatest names in Norwich City's history.

Reg Foulkes, a centre-half, made his City debut at the beginning of the 1950/51 season on 19 August at home to Port Vale. He made 238 appearances, scoring 8 goals. Foulkes was captain of the side which finished second, third and fourth in his first three seasons.

Don Pickwick, a right-half, kicked off his City career at home to Watford on 30 August 1947, but played just 9 matches throughout his first season. He became a regular from the 1948/49 season and went on to amass a total of 244 games and 11 goals. In May 1956, he left City to join Spalding United as player-manager.

John Gavin, an outside-right and City's greatest ever marksmen. He scored 132 goals in 338 appearances for the club, making his debut at the end of the 1948/49 season at Bristol Rovers on 30 April. Gavin became top scorer in 1950/51 with 18 goals and was subsequently always amongst the leading goalscorers until his final season for City, in which he also top scored with 22 goals, 1957/58 – after which he joined Watford.

Noel Kinsey, an inside-right, made his debut at home against Watford on 30 August 1947 and made a total of 243 appearances, scoring 65 goals. He made 4 appearances for Wales whilst a Third Divsion player with City, and left to join Birmingham City in June 1953. He was City's top scorer in the 1949/50 season with 17 goals.

Roy Hollis, a centre forward, made a stunning debut for City, scoring a hat-trick in 30 minutes against Queens Park Rangers at the end of the 1947/48 season in the 5-2 home victory on 21 April 1948. He top scored in 1951/52 with 22 goals, including five against Walsall in a 8-0 home victory. He made 107 appearances for City, scoring 59 goals. Hollis joined Tottenham briefly in 1952 before moving on to Southend (returning with them to Carrow Road to score a hat-trick against City in a 3-3 draw).

Leslie Eyre, an inside or outside-left, made his City debut after the war at home to Crystal Palace on 26 September 1946 and was top scorer for his first two seasons with 18 goals in 1946/47 and 16 in 1947/48. He scored five against Brighton in a 7-2 FA Cup win at Carrow Road on 30 November 1946 and netted a total of 69 goals in 201 appearances for the Canaries before leaving in November 1951 for Bournemouth.

Thomas Docherty, an outside-left, made his City debut at the beginning of the 1950/51 Third Division (South) season at home to Port Vale on 19 August 1950. He played 92 matches for City, scoring 7 goals (including a brace in the giant-killing of Liverpool in the FA Cup win on 6 January 1951, when City won 3-1). Docherty left City to join Reading in July 1953.

Terence Ryder, an outside right, made his debut at Notts County on 14 September 1946. He went on to make a total of 51 appearances, scoring 12 times, before joining current First Division champions Portsmouth in October 1950 (although Pompey didn't challenge for the title that year, eventually finishing seventh).

Norwich City Football Club

ENGLISH LEAGUE DIVISION III (Southern)
and Football Combination

FIXTURES, 1951-52

With the Compliments of

STEWARD & PATTESON LTD.

Pockthorpe Brewery, Norwich

Telephone No.   Norwich 20501

Fixture List Copyright by the Football League Ltd.,
reproduced by kind permission of the Norwich City
Football Club

A fixture card from the 1951/52 season. For the second season running, City had finished close to the champions – but as only one club were promoted they had to try yet again. The 1951/52 season saw two high-scoring home wins, an 8-0 victory over Walsall on 29 December 1951 and a 7-0 win over Torquay United on 14 April 1952. They also hit five against Colchester United, Bristol City and Gillingham.

Norwich City played Arsenal in the third round of the FA Cup on 12 January 1952. It was the first encounter in the competition between the two teams, and for City it wasn't an enjoyable one – losing 5-0 at Carrow Road. The Canaries would have to wait a little longer for FA Cup glory. From left to right, back row: N. Low (manager), J. Gavin, B. Lewis, R. Hollis, R. Foulkes, K. Nethercott, R. Ashman, A. Ackerman, M. Proctor (trainer). Front row: D. Jones, D. Rackham, R. Morgan, N. Kinsey, L. Dutton.

The local newspaper, *The Pink 'Un*, looks forward to the visit of the famous Arsenal to Carrow Road for the FA Cup tie in January 1952.

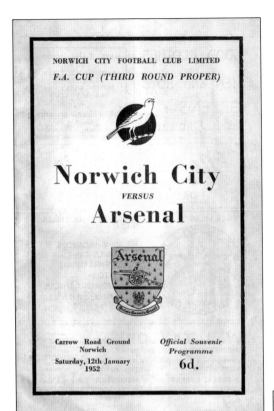

NORWICH CITY FOOTBALL CLUB LIMITED

F.A. CUP (THIRD ROUND PROPER)

Norwich City

VERSUS

Arsenal

Carrow Road Ground
Norwich

Saturday, 12th January
1952

*Official Souvenir
Programme*

6d.

The programme for the Norwich City *v* Arsenal FA Cup tie. Arsenal went on to reach the final, only to lose 1-0 to holders Newcastle United.

A souvenir 'pirate' programme for the Arsenal tie. These programmes were printed by an independent source and carried little or often no details of the game or players taking part, apart from the team line-ups.

CARROW ROAD GROUND
NORWICH

F. A. CUP

THIRD ROUND

NORWICH CITY

v

ARSENAL

Saturday, 12th January, 1952.
Kick-off 2 15 p.m.

SOUVENIR

PROGRAMME

Tom Johnston, a centre forward, made his debut for City at the beginning of the 1952/53 season on 23 August for a Third Division (South) match at home to Aldershot, in which he scored in a 5-0 victory. He scored 15 goals from 27 games during his first season, including four in his seventh match as City recorded an 8-1 win at Shrewsbury. He made a total of just 67 appearances for City, scoring 33 goals, before joining Newport County in October 1954. He later became a legend for Leyton Orient, netting 123 goals in 190 matches to become the O's seasonal and aggregate top scorer of all time.

A cartoon of City's 1953/54 FA Cup meeting at non-League Yeovil Town. The first round tie took place on 21 November 1953, before 11,760 spectators. City won 2-0 on Yeovil's famous sloping pitch.

City, as a Third Division (South) team, took revenge over First Division Arsenal for the 5-0 FA Cup defeat at Carrow Road two years earlier, with a fourth round giant-killing win at Highbury in front of 55,767 spectators on 30 January 1954, winning 2-1. Tom Johnston scored both Norwich goals after Arsenal had taken the lead. The Canaries went on to reach the fifth round before going down 2-1 at home to Second Division Leicester City (who were champions of their division that season). The cartoon is from the local paper, *The Pink 'Un*.

The handbook for the 1955/56 season, celebrating fifty years as a professional club. City supporters were looking forward to renewing their acquaintance with rivals Ipswich during the campaign, as the Suffolk side had been relegated from the Second Division at the end of the previous season. Norwich played both matches over the Easter Holiday period, losing 4-1 away on the Friday but finding revenge with a 3-2 home win the following Monday. City eventually finished seventh in the Third Division (South) that season.

NORWICH CITY FOOTBALL CLUB
50th Anniversary

Official Handbook

SEASON 1955-56

PRICE
1/-

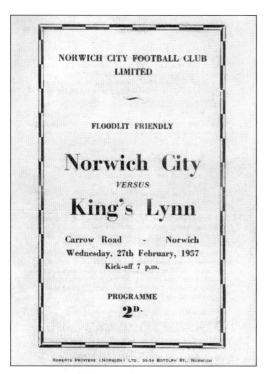

NORWICH CITY FOOTBALL CLUB
LIMITED

FLOODLIT FRIENDLY

Norwich City

VERSUS

King's Lynn

Carrow Road   -   Norwich
Wednesday, 27th February, 1957
Kick-off 7 p.m.

PROGRAMME
2ᴰ·

ROBERTS PRINTERS (NORWICH) LTD., 50-54 BOTOLPH ST., NORWICH

Norwich City *v*. Kings Lynn programme for
a floodlit friendly in aid of the City Appeal
Fund on Wednesday 27 February 1957. Ex-
City man Terry Ryder was a Kings Lynn
player who, according to the programme
notes, 'still seems to find the net regularly.'
City scored the most goals in this though,
winning 5-1. It was a different story in the
League, however, as City were to finish
bottom of the Third Division (South) for
the second time in their history.

Norfolk County Football Association

Chairman of the Council : A. MACK, Esq.

SENIOR CUP FINAL

NORWICH CITY v. KING'S LYNN

Carrow Road Ground, Norwich

EASTER MONDAY, APRIL 7th, 1958

Kick-off 11 a.m.

OFFICIAL PROGRAMME 3d.

Norwich City *v*. Kings Lynn programme for the 1957/58 Norfolk Senior Cup final on Monday 7
April 1958 at Carrow Road. Kings Lynn were the holders of the cup for the last four seasons and
won it again, defeating City's second team 3-1. Norwich City were to win it in the following two
seasons, however, defeating Gorleston 7-2 in 1958/59 and Kings Lynn 3-0 in 1959/60.

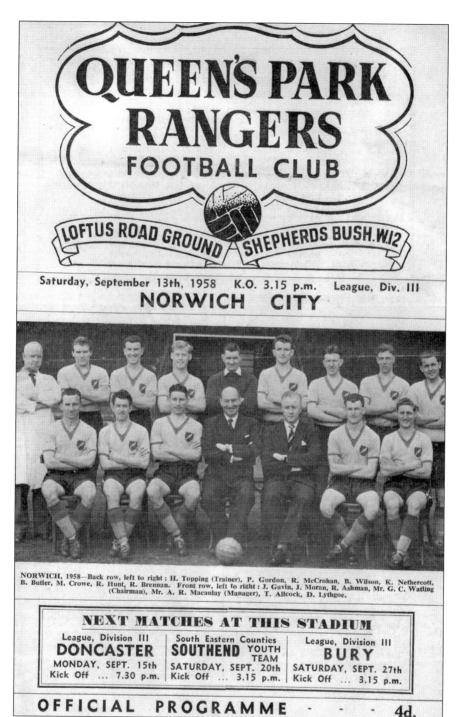

QUEEN'S PARK RANGERS
FOOTBALL CLUB

LOFTUS ROAD GROUND · SHEPHERDS BUSH. W.12

Saturday, September 13th, 1958   K.O. 3.15 p.m.   League, Div. III

NORWICH CITY

NORWICH, 1958—Back row, left to right: H. Topping (Trainer), P. Gordon, R. McCrohan, B. Wilson, K. Nethercott, B. Butler, M. Crowe, R. Hunt, R. Brennan. Front row, left to right: J. Gavin, J. Moran, R. Ashman, Mr. G. C. Watling (Chairman), Mr. A. R. Macaulay (Manager), T. Allcock, D. Lythgoe.

NEXT MATCHES AT THIS STADIUM

League, Division III	South Eastern Counties	League, Division III
DONCASTER	**SOUTHEND** YOUTH TEAM	**BURY**
MONDAY, SEPT. 15th Kick Off ... 7.30 p.m.	SATURDAY, SEPT. 20th Kick Off ... 3.15 p.m.	SATURDAY, SEPT. 27th Kick Off ... 3.15 p.m.

OFFICIAL PROGRAMME - - - 4d.

The programme from a Third Division match at Loftus road between City and Queens Park Rangers on 13 September 1958. The 1958/59 season was to go down in City's history as one of the club's finest. Although they finished fourth in the Third Division, it was their exploits in the FA Cup that would live on in people's memories. City lost this match at QPR 2-1.

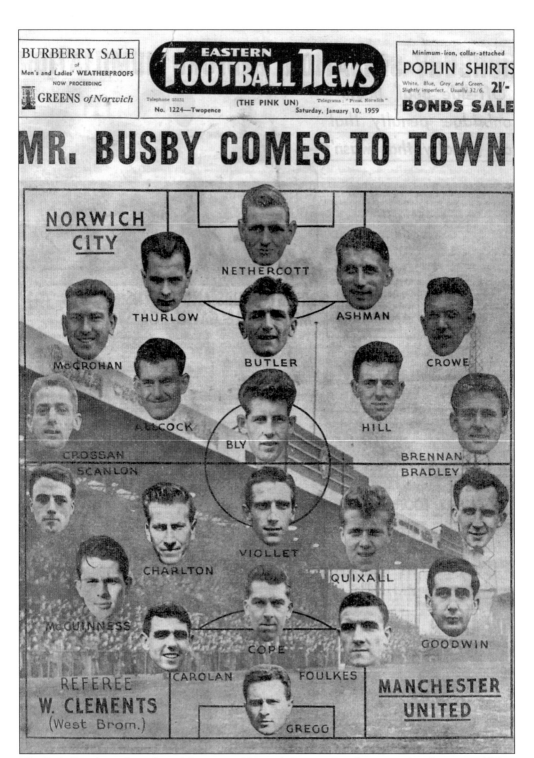

The Pink 'Un from Saturday 10 January 1959 and Carrow Road prepare for the visit of Matt Busby and his Manchester United team.

EASTERN
FOOTBALL NEWS

Telephone 23351
No. 1224—Twopence   (THE PINK UN)   Telegrams: " Press. Norwich
Saturday, January 10, 1959

BLY, BLY, BABES!

FIRST OF THE THREE

Spanked by great City

Bly puts City in the lead.

TERRY STARS AS THEY
ARE CUT DOWN TO SIZE

NORWICH CITY 3   MANCHESTER UTD. ... 0
Attendance 38,000—receipts £4500.

FANTASTIC ... superb ... all the superlatives are needed to describe Norwich City's tremendous Cup fight at Carrow Road this afternoon when a capacity crowd of 38,000 saw them grind Manchester United, football's " Red Devils," into the Norwich snow.

There was only one side in it—the City—and they had the man of the match in centre-forward Terry Bly. If Bly has not earned the freedom of Norwich tonight then 38,000 people will want to know why.

It was Bly who hammered home the first goal after half an hour when Bobby Brennan, just the man for the moment, flicked a cool pass back to him out of Gregg's hands.

It was Bly who, after an hour, belted in a right-footed drive that Gregg touched on to Crossan's head for the second goal, and it was Bly who, two minutes from time, made sure with a searing right-footed drive from a narrow angle that had Gregg hopelessly beaten.

Bly gave Cope, in the United defence, a thoroughly unhappy afternoon, but the City side as a whole rose to the occasion in tremendous fashion.

Suiting themselves much the better to the snowbound conditions City harried United unmercifully and thoroughly earned their reward—the defeat of last year's beaten Cup finalists, the ending of this year's second favourite's hopes of reaching Wembley for the third successive year and the wrecking of the Babes run of eight successive victories.

LIKE A DREAM

Manager Archie Macaulay's plan to minimise the threat that was likely from United's inside trio worked like a dream. Charlton and Quixall were never allowed the room in which to use their talent and the United side as a whole was marked out of the game.

So effective was City's defensive policy that Nethercott was seriously extended only once, when he dealt in grand style with a curling shot from Scanlon.

With their forwards so firmly held United looked a very ordinary team. Their wing-halves could never cope

SCOREBOARD

BLY (City) ...... 31 min.
CROSSAN (City) 61 min.
BLY (City) ...... 88 min.

with the splendid work of Hill and Allcock while neither Foulkes nor Carolan looked at all happy when Brennan and Crossan went on the rampage.

But above all this was Terry Bly's day and if he does nothing else all season he will have earned his laurels.

There was a big cheer as Foulkes led United on to the snowbound pitch and an even greater one as Ronnie Ashman, today equalling Joe Hannah's record of 431 appearances, led the Canaries out.

CITY—Nethercott; Thurlow, Ashman; Foulkes, Carolan; Goodwin, Cope, McGuinness; Bradley, Quixall, Viollet, Charlton, Scanlon.

MANCHESTER UNITED — Gregg; Foulkes, Carolan; Goodwin, Cope, McCrohan, Butler, Crowe; Crossan, Allcock, Bly, Hill, Brennan.

Referee—W. Clements (West Bromwich).

Ashman did his side a good turn by winning the toss and setting United to face the strong sun. It was obvious from the start, as the players skidded about, that the conditions were going to make play extremely difficult, but

Continued on page 4, col. 1

EVANS, LANGMAN WINNERS FOR COLCHESTER

CHESTERFIELD were first to attack at Layer Road and Fisher breasted a shot from Freer off the goal-line.

Colchester went ahead in their first real attack of the game in the eighth minute. There was a shot from EVANS, but the inside-left followed up smartly and forced the ball over the line.

The frozen pitch made good football impossible.

Langman had a chance for Colchester, but he squared the ball to a

EVENING MOURNING

Tables at the Grosvenor Rooms, Norwich, decorated in Manchester United colours for a dinner party for about 100 United supporters, were hastily draped with black when the result was known.

defender instead of taking advantage of a clear shot at goal.

Chesterfield continued to do most of the attacking, but Colchester looked more dangerous in their breakaways. Half-time:—

COLCHESTER 1
CHESTERFIELD 0

Colchester opened the second half with some well-spirited attacks and Banks did well to stop a shot from Evans.

Colchester pressed hard and in the 55th minute LANGMAN raced on to a back pass from centre-half Blakey and swept the ball past Banks to put Colchester further ahead.

Frear and Lewis created several good chances for Chesterfield, but although they fought back splendidly they could not reduce the arrears.

Oblion missed an excellent chance before an empty goal and Hammond cleared a shot from Lewis off the goal line. But at the other end Colchester attacked brilliantly and always looked dangerous. Result:—

COLCHESTER 2
CHESTERFIELD 0

Combination

Cardiff Res. 1, Orient Res. 1.
Reading Res. 2, Bournemouth Res. 0.
Swansea Res. 1, Birmingham Res. 5.
Watford Res. 4, Aldershot Res. 0.

Scores at a Glance

League Tables on Back Page.

F.A. CUP
(Third Round)

				H.T.
Accrington ..3	0	Darlingt'n ..2-0	
Aston V. ...2	1	Roth'rh'm ..0-0	
Barrow 2	4	Wolves 1-1	
Blackburn 4	2	Leyton O. ..1-0	
Brentford ..2	0	Barnsley 1-0	
Brighton ...2	0	Bradf'd C. ..0-1	
Bristol R. ..0	4	Charlton ...0-3	
Bury 0	1	Arsenal 0-0	
Colchester .2	0	Chesterf'd ..1-0	
Derby 2	2	Preston 2-1	
Everton 4	0	Sunderl'd ..2-0	
Fulham 0	0	Peterbro' ...0-0	
Grimsby ...2	2	Manch'r C. ..2-0	
Ipswich 1	0	Huddersf'd 1-0	
Leicester ..1	1	Lincoln 0-1	
Luton 5	1	Leeds 0-0	
Middlesbro' 1	1	Birm'h'm ..0-1	

(Abandoned after 80 minutes)

Newport ...0	0	Torquay ...0-0	
NORWICH ..3	0	Manch'r U. 1-0	
Plymouth ..0	3	Cardiff 0-0	
Portsm'th ..3	1	Swansea ...1-1	
Scunth'pe ..2	2	Bolton 0-0	
Sheff'ld U. .2	2	Crystal P. ..0-0	
South'ton ..1	2	Blackpool ..1-2	
Stoke 5	1	Oldham 4-1	
Tottenham ..2	0	West Ham ..1-0	
Tooting & M.2	2	Nottm. F. ..2-0	

POSTPONED—Doncaster v Bristol City, Newcastle v Chelsea, Sheffield Wednesday v W.B.A., Stockport v Burnley, Worcester v Liverpool.

SCOTTISH LEAGUE: Div. II

Albion R. ...6	2	Stenh'sm'r..2-0	
Berwick 3	1	Arbroath ...0-1	
Cowdenb'th 1	5	Ayr Utd. ...0-4	
Dundee U. ..2	1	Dumb'ton ..1-1	
Forfar 1	1	E. Stirling ..0-0	
Stranraer ..1	3	Brechin 0-1	

POSTPONED—Alloa v Hamilton, Morton v East Fife, Queen's Park v St. Johnstone.

SNOWDRIFTS ON A140

The R.A.C. said this afternoon that snowdrifts on the A140 Cromer to Norwich road were causing single line traffic only between Roughton and Hanworth.

DIVISION III

				H.T.
Hull City ...3	2	Southend ..1-1	
Notts Co. ...3	1	Reading 2-0	
Swindon 0	1	B'mouth 0-1	

POSTPONED—Wrexham v Q.P.R.

DIVISION IV

Aldershot ..0	0	Crewe 0-0	
Millwall ...3	0	North't'n ..1-0	
Shrewsb'y ..0	1	Bradford ...0-1	

POSTPONED—Carlisle v Watford, Coventry v Port Vale, Gillingham v Chester, Walsall v Workington.

SCOTTISH LEAGUE. Div. I

Clyde 2	2	Stirling A. ..0-0	
Falkirk 0	2	Partick T. ..0-1	
Kilmarnock 1	0	Dundee 0-0	
Queen o' S. .1	4	Hibernian ..0-2	

POSTPONED—Aberdeen v Third Lanark, Hearts v St. Mirren, Motherwell v Dunfermline, Raith v Celtic, Rangers v Airdrie.

Nethercott punches clear a free kick that provided one of United's few dangerous moments.

The same day and a later edition reveals that it's Manchester United who are out of the FA Cup.

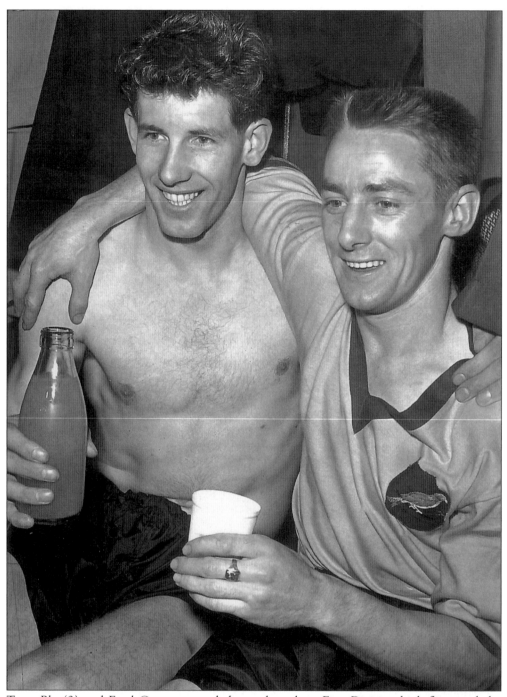

Terry Bly (2) and Errol Crossan scored the goals to beat First Division high-fliers and the previous season's beaten FA Cup finalists, Manchester United. The 3-0 win at Carrow Road took place on a snow-laden pitch before a packed 38,000 crowd.

The famous 1958/59 FA Cup team (apart from Sandy Kennon, who was to replace the injured Nethercott for the Sheffield United replay and the two semi-final matches). From left to right, back row: R. McCrohan, B. Thurlow, K. Nethercott, B. Butler, R. Ashman, M. Crowe. Front row: E. Crossan, T. Allcock, T. Bly, J. Hill, B. Brennan. City played eleven FA Cup matches during that epic run: Ilford (h) 3-1; Swindon (a) 1-1, (h) 1-0; Manchester United (h) 3-0; Cardiff City (h) 3-2; Tottenham (a) 1-1, (h) 1-0; Sheffield United (a) 1-1, (h) 3-2; Luton Town (at White Hart Lane) 1-1, (at St Andrews, Birmingham) 0-1.

All smiles in the dressing room after another cup victory. This time Norwich have beaten Second Division Cardiff City 3-2 in the fourth round on 24 January 1959 in front of another capacity crowd of 38,000 at Carrow Road.

Captain Ron Ashman celebrates after another glorious win in the 1959 FA Cup run.

The Norwich City *v.* Manchester United programme for the 1959 FA Cup encounter at Carrow Road.

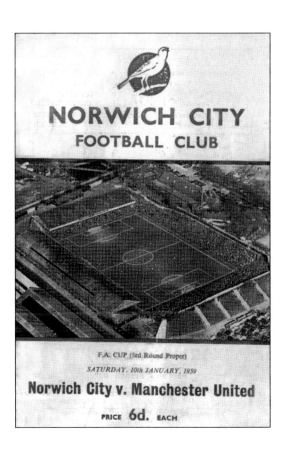

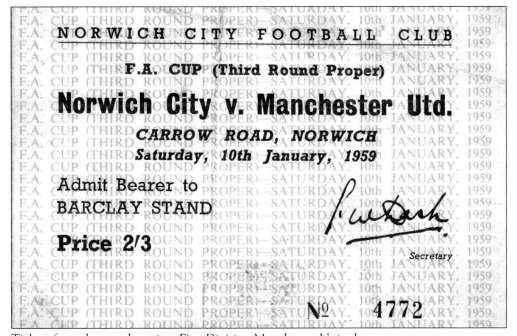

Tickets from the match against First Division Manchester United.

EASTERN
Football News
Telephone 85631
No. 1229—Twopence
(THE PINK UN)
Telegrams : "Press, Norwich."
Saturday, February 14, 1959

WOTCHA, COCK!

TOTTENHAM HOTSPUR

HOLLOWBREAD

BAKER   HOPKINS

DODGE   NORMAN   ILEY

BROOKS   HARMER   SMITH   DUNMORE   JONES

Referee : J. W. Topliss   (Grimsby)

BRENNAN   HILL   BLY   ALLCOCK   CROSSAN

CROWE   BUTLER   McCROHAN

ASHMAN   THURLOW

NETHERCOTT

NORWICH CITY

The Pink 'Un looks forward to the Spurs clash in the fifth round on 14 February at White Hart Lane.

68

A Sheffield newspaper, *The Star*, looks ahead to the semi-finals before the day's quarter-final meeting between Sheffield United and Norwich. Erroll Crossnan equalised at Bramell Lane for a 1-1 draw to set up another thrilling cup replay at Carrow Road. It was a day of heroism as 'keeper Ken Nethercott played on in the last half hour of the match with a dislocated shoulder. He was replaced by Sandy Kennon in goal for the replay, which City won 3-2 with Terry Bly scoring twice and a goal from Bobby Brennan allowing Norwich to reach the semi-final for the first time in the club's history.

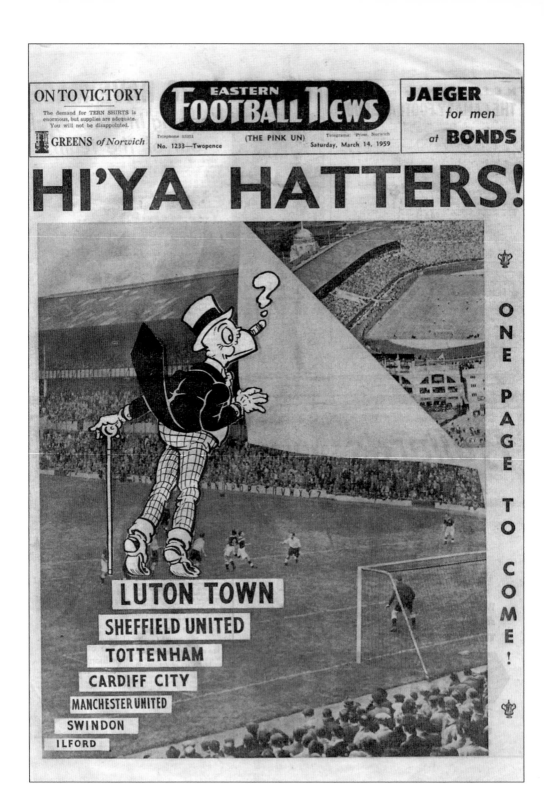

The Pink 'Un from the day of the semi-final clash with First Division Luton Town at White Hart Lane.

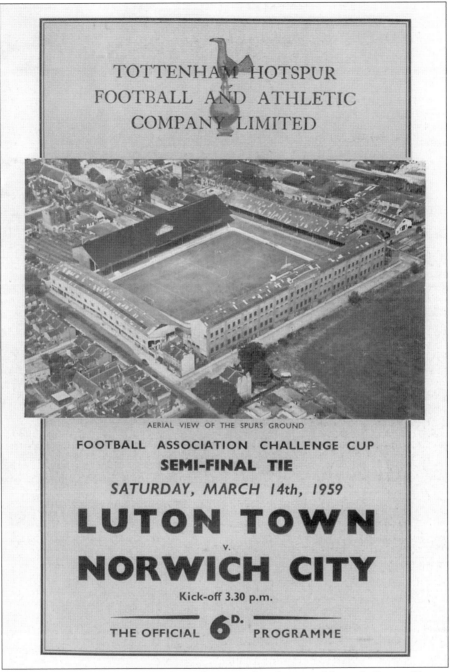

TOTTENHAM HOTSPUR
FOOTBALL AND ATHLETIC
COMPANY LIMITED

AERIAL VIEW OF THE SPURS GROUND

FOOTBALL ASSOCIATION CHALLENGE CUP
SEMI-FINAL TIE
SATURDAY, MARCH 14th, 1959

LUTON TOWN
v.
NORWICH CITY

Kick-off 3.30 p.m.

THE OFFICIAL **6**D. PROGRAMME

The programme for the semi-final at White Hart lane between Norwich City and Luton Town. A crowd of 63,500 saw a 1-1 draw, with Bobby Brennan equalising for City in the 65th minute to ensure that the Canaries' dream of becoming the very first club from the Third Division to reach the Cup Final lived on. Although City finished fourth in the Division Three table that season, they were actually in thirteenth place on the day of the semi-final, with sixteen matches left to play. Meanwhile, Nottingham Forest won the other semi-final by beating Aston Villa 1-0 to await the replay winners at Wembley.

EASTERN FOOTBALL NEWS

(THE PINK UN)

No. 1233—Twopence   Telephone 82351   Telegrams: "Press, Norwich"   Saturday, March 14, 1959

IT'S A REPLAY

Brennan birthday goal keeps City there

KENNON PLAYED HERO'S GAME FOR NORWICH

NORWICH CITY 1   LUTON TOWN 1

NORWICH CITY AND LUTON HAVE GOT TO GO THROUGH IT ALL AGAIN AT ST. ANDREW'S, BIRMINGHAM, ON WEDNESDAY — THANKS TO A BIRTHDAY GOAL BY BRENNAN.

But salute Sandy Kennon, who made two out-of-this-world saves towards the end of this afternoon's Cup Semi-Final at White Hart Lane, to give the Canaries another opportunity of becoming the first Third Division side to reach the Final.

Kennon completely dispelled any doubts there might have been about his ability as Nethercott's deputy. Brilliant does not describe those two saves that stopped Bingham from giving Luton a decisive lead towards the end of this titanic battle.

They were uncanny, the saves of a 'keeper at the peak of his form and on this display, one of the best in the world.

But salute the City team as a whole, too, for their tremendous fight-back after a first-half in which it seemed that Luton were going almost to stroll to victory. Allan Brown headed the First Division club into the lead in the 35th minute, and but for the sterling work of Kennon and the men in front of him, they must have been more than a goal up at the interval.

But the second-half was a different demons. Using the wings they had largely neglected in the first half, they flung themselves against the wall of Luton's defence, and 20 minutes into the second half McCrohan crossed the ball from whom Brennan lashed home a golden equaliser to celebrate his 20th birthday.

One to remember

City found Luton a far different proposition from what they probably expected and in particular it took them all their time to keep a watch on Bingham on the right wing. Apart, however, the Luton attack was well held.

But City, too, did not find the attacking going easy. Crowan, after the interval, failed to maintain first-half promise and Bly, who seemed a trifle overawed by the occasion, never really got the better of Owen.

But for excitement, this was a game that City supporters will remember all their lives.

The City party is due to return to Norwich this evening on the East Anglian at 6.30 from Liverpool Street, arriving about 9.35.

There was consternation in the Norwich camp when it was read in the official programme that extra time would be played if scores were level after 90 minutes.

It was not until chairman Geoffrey Watling and manager Archie Macaulay approached the secretary of the Football Association, Sir Stanley Rous, that the position was cleared up.

Sir Stanley said that it was a mistake. The programme about extra time referred to any possible replay at Birmingham next week and if the scores were level after an hour and a-half today, that would be that until Wednesday.

It was obvious that City's supporters had profited from their previous visit to Tottenham, for they seemed to have occupied every vantage point inside the ground.

Wherever one looked there were the green-and-yellow favours of Norwich followers, and, as one spectator remarked, "A few Luton people seem to have got here as well."

The Norwich masses had been augmented for the occasion and as they parade the ground they outnumbered

Luton's representatives by something like 10 to 1. There were even women mascots on this occasion, one of them draped in a flowing green and yellow robe.

And despite the efforts of the Tottenham band, there was no drowning the strains of City's battle chant. 'On the Ball, City' swelled from the terraces time and again as the band stopped their efforts for a moment or two.

Huge roar

Although their supporters seemed to be in a minority, Luton got a rousing cheer when their veteran centre-half, Sid Owen, led them on to the field.

But it was nothing to the roar that greeted the Canaries on their appearance. And no sooner had the roar died down than the strains of " On the Ball, City " resounded once more around the packed terraces.

It was not until less than half an hour before the start that Luton announced that Gregory would be at outside-left and not Adams.

Gregory, who entered the Forces last week, has been receiving treatment for a thigh muscle pull throughout the week, but Luton obviously decided that he was fit enough to take his place in the side.

As usual Athman kept the referee and Owen waiting for a few seconds before moving to the middle for the toss. While Owen was spinning the coin there was a chorus of "Happy

Continued on Page 6, Col. 1

LINE UP

NORWICH CITY

Kennon

Thurlow   Ashman

McCrohan   Butler   Crowe

Crossan   Allcock   Bly   Hill   Brennan

Gregory   Cummins   Morton   Brown   Bingham

Pacey   Owen   Groves

Hawkes   McNally

Baynham

LUTON TOWN

Referee: W. HICKSON (Wigan)

NORWICH EQUALISE — Brennan's shot flashes into the net for the equaliser.

LUTON SCORE — Brown (on right) falls after heading the ball home.

F.A. CUP AND LEAGUE RESULTS

F.A. CUP—Semi-finals

			H.T.
NORWICH ..1	1 Luton	0-1	
Nottm. F. ..1	0 Aston V.	0-0	

DIVISION I

Arsenal 1	1 Blackb'rn	0-1	
Birm'h'm ..0	3 Wolves	0-2	
Burnley 1	0 West Ham	0-0	
Everton 3	1 Blackpool	2-0	
Leeds 1	3 Tottenham	1-0	
Leicester ...0	3 Chelsea	0-0	
Man. City ..5	1 Newcastle	2-1	
W.B.A. 1	3 Man. Utd.	0-3	

DIVISION II

Bristol R. ..4	1 Rotherh'm	1-0	
Derby 1	1 Sheff. Utd.	2-0	
Fulham 3	2 Middlesbro	1-0	
Ipswich 3	1 Barnsley	2-1	
Leyton O. ..3	2 Brighton	0-1	
Lincoln 3	3 Charlton	2-2	
Scunth'pe ..3	3 Grimsby	1-1	
Stoke 0	1 Cardiff	0-0	
Sund'rl'd ...3	1 Bristol C.	0-1	
Swansea 0	1 Huddersf'd	0-0	

DIVISION III

			H.T.
Accringt'n ..0	2 Bury	0-1	
Brad. City ..0	1 B'mouth	0-0	
Brentford ...3	1 Reading	2-1	
Doncaster ..3	1 Chester'd	1-1	
Halifax 3	1 Q.P.R.	1-1	
Hull 3	0 Colchester	1-0	
Mansfield ..0	2 Tranmere	0-0	
Notts Co. ...1	2 Plymouth	1-2	
South'ton ..3	2 Southend	2-1	
Swindon 3	0 Stockport	0-0	
Newport v Rochdale (late kick-off)			

DIVISION IV

Aldershot ..2	4 Hartlep'ls	1-2	
Barrow 1	0 Palace	1-0	
Carlisle 0	3 Port Vale	0-1	
Coventry ...4	0 Working'n	1-0	
Darlingt'n ..1	1 Crewe	0-1	
Exeter 0	2 York	0-1	
Gatesh'd ...1	0 Watford	1-0	
Gillingh'm ..1	1 Bradford	1-0	
Millwall 1	1 Southport	0-0	
Oldham 3	5 Chester	2-4	
Shrews'y ...2	0 North'n	2-0	
Walsall 2	2 Torquay	1-2	

SCOTTISH CUP

(FOURTH ROUND)

			R.T.
Aberdeen ..3	1 Kilmarnock	2-1	
St. Mirren ..2	1 Dunf'line	1-0	
Stirling A. ..1	3 Celtic	0-3	
T. Lanark ..1	1 Hibernian	0-2	

SCOTTISH LEAGUE. Div. I

Clyde 2	2 Hearts	1-0	
Dundee 2	1 Queen o'S	1-1	
Falkirk 5	5 Rangers	4-2	

SCOTTISH LEAGUE. Div. II

Alloa 4	2 E. Stirling	1-0	
Arbroath 1	3 Ayr Utd.	1-1	
Berwick 1	4 Stenh'sm'r	0-3	
Cowd'n'th ..6	0 Dundee U	1-0	
Hamilton 3	4 Brechin	0-3	
Montrose ...1	1 Albion R	0-0	
Morton 4	1 Forfar	1-1	
Queen's P. ..3	2 Stranraer	0-0	
St. John's'n ..6	1 E. Fife	3-0	

Amateur International

Scotland 1	1 England	1-0	

A group of City supporters celebrate, with First Division Luton Town next on the agenda.

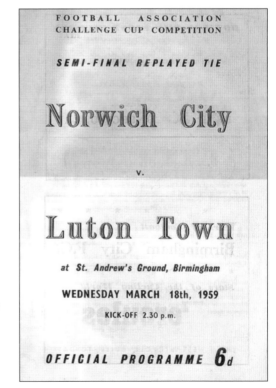

FOOTBALL   ASSOCIATION
CHALLENGE CUP COMPETITION

SEMI-FINAL REPLAYED TIE

Norwich City

v.

Luton Town

at St. Andrew's Ground, Birmingham

WEDNESDAY MARCH 18th, 1959

KICK-OFF 2.30 p.m.

OFFICIAL PROGRAMME 6d

The Norwich City *v.* Luton Town FA Cup semi-final replay programme for the game at St Andrews, Birmingham. A crowd of 49,500 saw Luton win 1-0 with a Bingham goal after 56 minutes (Luton lost the final 2-1 to Nottingham Forest).

CANARY
CRUSADE

Edited by TED BELL, Sports Editor,
"Eastern Daily Press" and
"Eastern Evening News"

PRICE
2/-

A thirty-two page book was produced as a tribute to the achievements of the team during 1958/59. The front cover pictures, from left to right: Butler, Crossan, Crowe, Brennan, Hill, Bly, Kennon, Allcock, McCrohan, Ashman. Inset: Nethercott and Thurlow.

74

Four

Promotion Seasons and the League Cup

The 1959/60 team. From left to right, back row: B. Thurlow, T. Allcock, R. McCrohan, S. Kennon, B. Butler, T. Bly, M. Crowe, H. Topping. Front row: E. Crossan, J. Hill, B. Whitehouse, R. Ashman, B. Larkin, R. Brennan, B. Punton. Norwich at last won promotion back to the Second Divsion – in which they had not played since just before the Second World War. The team finished as runners-up, 2 points behind champions Southampton. There was to be no repeat of FA Cup glory, however, as fellow Third Division side Reading knocked City out 2-1 in a first round replay.

Bill Punton in action against Newport County on 24 October 1959 in a Third Division match that City won 1-0.

The match that virtually clinched promotion – City players celebrate at Queens Park Rangers on 23 April 1960 after a goalless draw. City won their final two matches, which were both at home, 4-3 against Southend United and 3-0 against Chesterfield to secure second place and promotion back to the Second Division for Archie Macaulay's side.

Cartoon from *The Pink 'Un* on 30 April 1960 after City's promotion back to the Second Division.

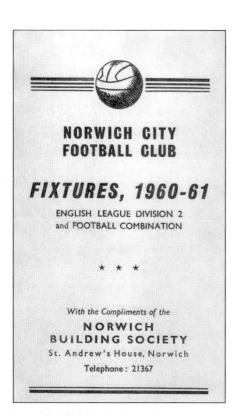

The fixture card for 1960/61. City were to have a good season, finishing fourth behind Liverpool and reaching the fifth round of the FA Cup, eventually losing 0-1 at home to Sunderland.

Bill Punton, sandwiched between two defenders, puts a shot just wide of the post, beating Southampton 'keeper Godfrey during the last game of the 1960/61 season. The mach on 29 April 1961 at Carrow Road ended 5-0 in City's favour and Bill was amongst the scorers.

Ron Ashman, the City captain, making his 100th successive appearance for the second time in his Norwich career. The match on 4 February 1961 at Lincoln City ended 4-1 in City's favour and this picture shows Ron shaking hands with the Lincoln City captain, Middleton – who was, coincidentally, making his first 100th successive appearance for Lincoln.

Bill Punton, a left winger, joined City from Southend United in 1959 and made his debut on 31 August 1959 at Tranmere Rovers in a Third Division match. He helped City to win promotion to the Second Division and win the League Cup in 1962, scoring in the 3-0 win at Rochdale in the first leg and also playing in the second leg, which City won 1-0. He made a total of 256 appearances, scoring 29 goals, before leaving the club in 1966 to join Sheffield United.

The Norwich City 1961/62 team. From left to right, back row: Sutton, Scott, Hill, Thurlow, Mannion, Waites, Lythgoe, Savino, Worrell, Williamson. Third row: Burton, Conway, Mullett, Allcock, Kennon, Barnsley, Applegate, Dowe, Butler, Nixon, Whitehouse, McCrohan, Parnell, Crowe. Second row: Punton, Cann (coach), Westwood (secretary), Hanly (director), Robinson (director), Watling (chairman), Fish (vice-chairman), Jex (director), Reid (team manager), Montgomery (trainer-coach), Ashman. Front row: Lloyd, Price, Turner, Howlett.

'Top Brass Special' – Norwich City Football Club supporters had a day out to First Division Sheffield United on 17 February 1962 for a fifth round FA Cup tie. City were dreaming of more FA Cup glory after beating First Division Ipswich Town (who were on their way to winning the Championship) 2-1 at Portman Road, but City lost at Sheffield 3-1. City also reached the quarter-finals in the following season, but lost 2-0 at home to Leicester in front of a record home crowd of 43,984.

Cup glory did arrive in 1961/62, with manager Willie Reid taking his team to their first national trophy success by winning the recently formed Football League Cup. The competition was only in its second year when City beat Chesterfield, Lincoln, Middlesbrough, Sunderland and (their only First Division opponents) Blackpool in the two-legged semi-final, before overwhelming Fourth Division Rochdale 4-0 in a two-legged final. City won 3-0 at Rochdale on 26 April 1962 with goals from Derrick Lythgoe (2) and Bill Punton in front of a crowd of 11,123 and 1-0 at Carrow Road on 1 May 1962 in front of 19,800, with Jimmy Hill scoring.

A history of Norwich City FC as seen by the *Rover & Adventure* comic.

Norwich City line-up in 1963/64 from a Typhoo Tea card collection. Goalkeeping legend Kevin Keelan made his debut for City at the start of the 1963/64 season, but shared goalkeeping duties with Sandy Kennon until he made the number 1 shirt his own towards the end of 1964.

Barry Butler was a fine centre-half. Tragically, on Saturday 9 April 1966 Barry died from injuries sustained in a car crash. He had made 349 appearances for City, scoring 3 goals since his first match on 24 August 1957 at home to Crystal Palace. He was a regular member of the City side, playing up until October 1965. This photograph shows a tribute to Barry by both teams on the Monday following his fatal accident, 11 April 1966, at Carrow Road, Rotherham United being City's opponents.

On 18 February 1967, Norwich went to Old Trafford in the fourth round of The FA Cup and beat the League Champions elect 2-1, with goals from Don Heath and Gordon Bollard. These photographs show City centre-half Laurie Brown clearing under pressure from Denis Law. This result meant that United had now only won once in three FA Cup ties with Norwich, winning in 1906 but losing to City in 1959 and 1967.

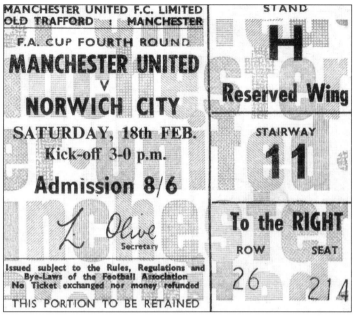

Ticket for the Manchester United *v.* Norwich City cup-tie on 18 February 1967.

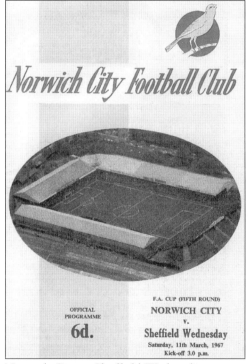

Norwich City *v.* Sheffield Wednesday programme for the FA Cup fifth round tie on 11 March 1967. First Division Sheffield Wednesday were beaten finalists the previous season and came to Carrow Road and won 3-1 in front of a crowd of 41,000. Also shown here is a pirate souvenir programme for the same match.

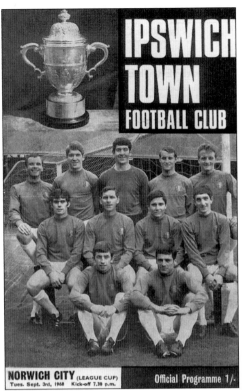

Programme for the Ipswich Town *v*. Norwich City Football League Cup second round tie on 3 September 1968. Second Division Norwich travelled down the road to their First Division neighbours and came back with a superb 4-2 victory, Hugh Curran scoring a hat-trick.

Hugh Curran scoring in the 4-2 demolition of First Division Ipswich at Portman Road in 1968.

Terry Allcock joined City from Bolton Wanderers in 1958, making his debut against Millwall at Carrow Road on 15 March. He made a total of 384 appearances, scoring 127 goals – making him City's number two all-time top goalscorer. Nicknamed 'The Count' he became youth team manager and chief coach after his playing days were over. His testimonial against Ipswich Town on 30 April 1969 ended 3-1 to City.

Mal Lucas, a right-half, joined City from Leyton Orient and made his debut on 16 September 1964 at home to Manchester City. He made 201 appearances for Norwich, scoring 10 goals, before leaving the club in March 1970 for Torquay United.

Duncan Forbes leads out his team at Brisbane Road, home of Orient, for a Second Division clash on 24 April 1972, with promotion to the First Division only a win away. Forbes made 350 appearances for City, scoring 12 goals. He had made his debut in 1968 and went on to serve the club as promotions and travel manager and then chief scout up to his retirement in 2001.

David Cross celebrates as Ken Foggo's shot beats Orient 'keeper Ray Goddard. A penalty from Graham Paddon secured a 2-1 victory and promotion.

Graham Paddon and Ken Foggo celebrate the win at Brisbane Road, 24 April 1972.

Two days after City were crowned Second Division champions at Watford, a celebration match in aid of the Fisherman's Fund was played against Lowestoft Town. City won 6-0 and the programme for the match was a single sheet costing 1p.

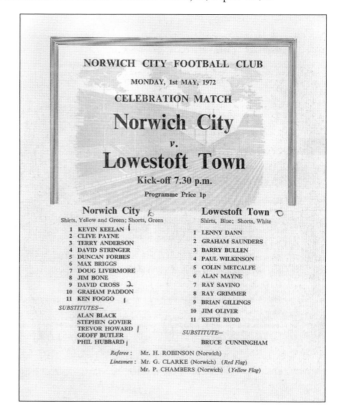

NORWICH CITY FOOTBALL CLUB

MONDAY, 1st MAY, 1972

CELEBRATION MATCH

Norwich City

v.

Lowestoft Town

Kick-off 7.30 p.m.

Programme Price 1p

Norwich City	Lowestoft Town
Shirts, Yellow and Green; Shorts, Green	Shirts, Blue; Shorts, White
1 KEVIN KEELAN	1 LENNY DANN
2 CLIVE PAYNE	2 GRAHAM SAUNDERS
3 TERRY ANDERSON	3 BARRY BULLEN
4 DAVID STRINGER	4 PAUL WILKINSON
5 DUNCAN FORBES	5 COLIN METCALFE
6 MAX BRIGGS	6 ALAN MAYNE
7 DOUG LIVERMORE	7 RAY SAVINO
8 JIM BONE	8 RAY GRIMMER
9 DAVID CROSS	9 BRIAN GILLINGS
10 GRAHAM PADDON	10 JIM OLIVER
11 KEN FOGGO	11 KEITH RUDD
SUBSTITUTES—	
ALAN BLACK	SUBSTITUTE—
STEPHEN GOVIER	
TREVOR HOWARD	BRUCE CUNNINGHAM
GEOFF BUTLER	
PHIL HUBBARD	

Referee : Mr. H. ROBINSON (Norwich)

Linesmen : Mr. G. CLARKE (Norwich) *(Red Flag)*
Mr. P. CHAMBERS (Norwich) *(Yellow Flag)*

Newspaper special celebrating the championship, as issued by *Eastern Counties Newspapers*.

Norwich City chairman Mr Geoffrey Watling presents Dave Stringer with the 1971/72 Barry Butler Player of the year trophy and replica trophy at Carrow Road. David Stringer made a total of 497 appearances for the club, scoring 22 goals. He had made his debut for City on 10 April 1965 at Coventry City. He is third in the all-time appearances list for the club. Stringer went on to manage the youth team from 1980 and later became reserve team manager, assistant manager to Ken Brown and then manager after Ken Brown's dismissal in November 1987, with the club struggling at the bottom of the First Division. At this time, Mike Walker had joined the club as the new reserve team manager and eventually took over from David Stringer for the new FA Premiership season in 1992/93.

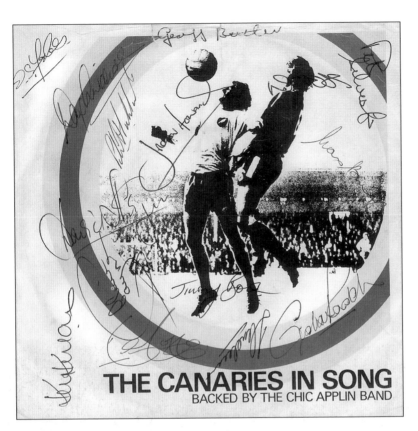

THE CANARIES IN SONG
BACKED BY THE CHIC APPLIN BAND

NORWICH CITY FOOTBALL SUPPORTERS
ASSOCIATION

PROMOTION
DINNER DANCE &
CABARET

SOUVENIR MENU

WEDNESDAY, MAY 10th, 1972

NORWOOD ROOMS, NORWICH

Kick-off 8 p.m.

Souvenirs from 1972. *Above*: A record written by supporters Don Shepherd and Johnny Cleveland, members of The Chic Applin Band, to celebrate City's rise to the First Division. *Left*: The souvenir menu from the promotion dinner dance held at the Norwood rooms on 10 May 1972. The music was provided by Chic Applin and his band.

Five
First Division Football and Wembley

Manager Ron Saunders and captain Duncan Forbes lead the City team out onto the Wembley turf for the first time in the club's history on 3 March 1973 to meet fellow First Division side Tottenham Hotspur.

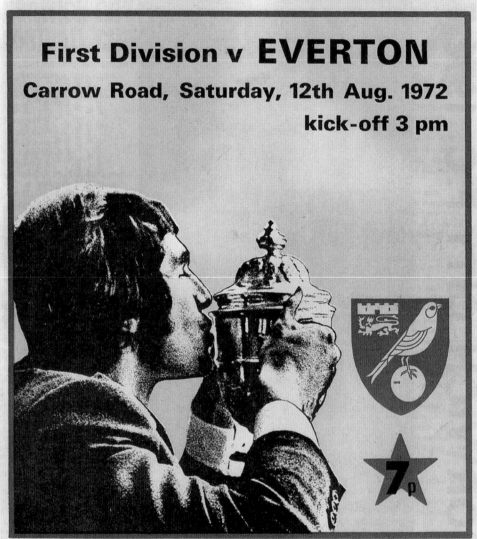

NORWICH CITY
FOOTBALL CLUB

First Division v EVERTON

Carrow Road, Saturday, 12th Aug. 1972

kick-off 3 pm

7p

Official Match-day Programme   Volume 1 Number 1

The first programme from the top flight. On 12 August 1972, Everton became City's inaugural opponents in a First Division match played in front of a crowd of 25,851. The game finished as a 1-1 draw, City's goalscorer was Jimmy Bone.

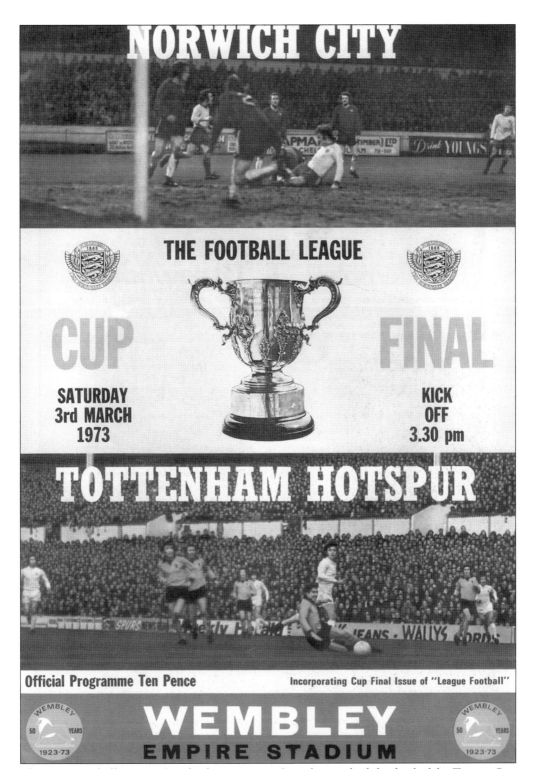

The 1973 Football League Cup final programme. City also reached the final of the Texaco Cup that season, but lost 4-2 on aggregate to Ipswich Town.

Bill Nicholson and Ron Saunders lead their teams out at Wembley in 1973.

Chelsea had knocked City out of the League Cup at the fifth round stage in 1971/72, but in the following season the Canaries got their revenge with a 3-0 aggregate win in the semi-finals to reach Wembley for the first time in their history. The match against the Blues at Stamford Bridge on 13 December 1972 ended 2-0 to City, with Jimmy Bone and David Cross scoring. The second leg at Carrow Road caused a bit of a scare for supporters as City led 3-2 (5-2 on aggregate), when the match was abandoned by referee Gordon Hill due to heavy fog with just six minutes remaining. City won the rematch at Carrow Road 1-0 with a Steve Govier goal.

Duncan Forbes is getting a header in with Martin Peters, Alan Gilzean and Mike England in attendance for Spurs. City lost 1-0 to a goal from Spurs substitute Ralph Coates.

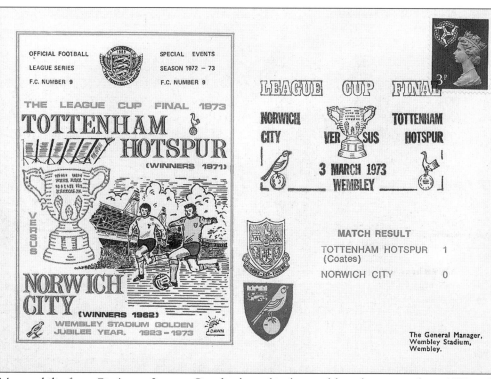

Memorabilia from City's two League Cup finals in the shape of first-day covers from 1973 and 1975. City were also beaten semi-finalists in 1974.

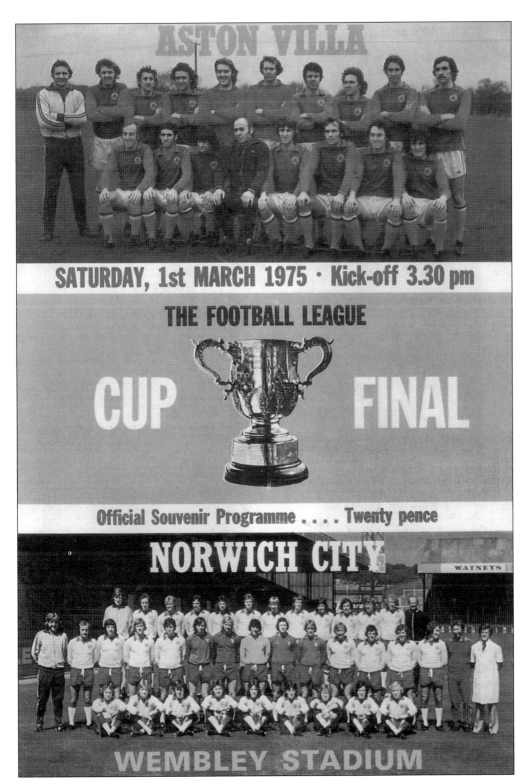

The programme for the 1975 League Cup final.

NORWICH CITY FOOTBALL CLUB

Celebration

THE NORWOOD ROOMS
NORWICH

LEAGUE CUP FINAL
1st MARCH 1975

The brochure for the celebration banquet to mark City's 1975 League Cup final appearance.

The 1975 League Cup final with Aston Villa ended in despair for City with a 1-0 defeat. Ron Saunders was now manager of Aston Villa and it was John Bond who led the City team out this time. In this photograph, Mel Machin handles on the goal line in spectacular fashion to concede a penalty which Ray Graydon converted past Kevin Keelan after the 'keeper had at first saved the kick only to see the rebound fall straight to Graydon via a post.

Phil Boyer, a striker, joined City in 1970 from Bournemouth for a club record fee of £145,000. He made his debut for Norwich on 9 February 1974 against Sheffield United in a First Division match. City were relegated at the end of the 1973/74 season, but Boyer, along with Ted MacDougal, formed a top-scoring partnership in 1974/75, with 33 League goals between them to help City bounce back at the first attempt. Boyer left City in 1977 for Southampton, having made a total of 139 appearances for City, scoring 40 goals.

Ted MacDougal was a prolific goalscorer who joined City from West Ham United in 1973. He made his City debut on 8 December 1973 at Burnley in a First Division match. MacDougal finished the season as top scorer for the club, and again in 1974/75 and 1975/76. He left for Southampton in September 1976 and finished on a total of 138 appearances for Canaries with 66 goals.

Kevin Keelan made his City debut at the beginning of the 1963/64 season on 24 August at Cardiff City in a Second Division match and shared goalkeeping duties with the previous first choice 'keeper, Sandy Kennon, for two seasons. In 1965/66 he was an ever-present and again in 1971/72, City's promotion season; he missed just one game during Norwich's first season in the First Division (a Texaco cup match at Dundee). Keelan played in both Wembley League Cup finals and finally left the club in February 1980 to go to the United States. Keelan made a total of 673 appearances for City and holds the top spot for all-time appearances for the club. He is pictured receiving an award from chairman Sir Arthur South and former chairman Geoffrey Watling in 1979 for breaking Ron Ashman's previous club appearance record of 662.

Martin Peters, Norwich's former England international midfielder, in action with a certain Ipswich town manager, George Burley.

Martin Peters in action with Orient's Bobby Fisher in a Anglo-Scottish Cup tie at Carrow Road on 12 August 1978. The game ended goalless. Peters joined City from Tottenham towards the end of the 1974/75 season, making his City debut at Old Trafford on 15 March. His glory days had been with Spurs and England, and of course had won a League Cup winners medal against Norwich in 1973. Despite being past his prime, Peters still managed 50 goals in 231 City appearances, leaving to become player-coach of Sheffield United in August 1980.

Kevin Reeves, a striker, made his City debut on 15 January 1977 at Arsenal and became one of the country's most expensive players when Norwich sold him to Manchester City in March 1980 for £1 million. He made a total of 132 appearances for the Canaries, scoring 42 goals.

Norwich City 3 Liverpool 5 was the thrilling scoreline from this First Division match on 9 February 1980. This was goalkeeper Kevin Keelan's 673rd and final match for City. Justin Fashanu scored a scorcher of a goal and David Fairclough grabbed a hat-trick for Liverpool. City's other goals were scored by Martin Peters (above) and Kevin Reeves.

Norwich *v.* Ipswich Town League Cup match programme for a tie played on 8 October 1980. City lost this replay 3-1 and three days later manager John Bond left Norwich for Manchester City.

October 1980 and it's all change at City. Ex-player Dave Stringer returns to the club as youth team coach, joining new manager Ken Brown, who had just replaced John Bond. Mel Machin, who is also in the picture, became Ken Brown's assistant and chief coach. Unfortunately, City were relegated back to the Second Division by the end of the 1980/81 campaign.

Justin Fashanu, pictured here at Attleborough School, where he signed schoolboy forms with Norwich, made his City debut on 13 January 1979 at home to West Bromwich Albion and became City's second £1 million player when sold to Nottingham Forest in August 1981. He will be remembered for his many goals, especially the strike against Liverpool in the 5-3 home defeat in 1980, when he won the *Match of the Day* Goal of the Season competition and featured on the programme credits. He made 97 appearances for Norwich, scoring 40 goals. His younger brother, John, made just 6 appearances for City, going on to finally achieve a remarkable career with Wimbledon.

Keith Bertschin, a striker, joined Norwich in 1981 from Birmingham City, making his debut at the beginning of the 1981/82 season at Rotherham United in a Second Division match on 29 August. City had been relegated from the First Division in the previous campaign, but with 12 goals, Bertshin was top scorer in the League for City – which helped them regain their top-flight place at the first attempt, Bertschin scoring in each of the last five League matches. With 10 League goals from both Ross Jack and John Deehan, City finally finished third in the Second Division table. Bertschin made a total 136 appearances for City, scoring 38 goals.

Despite losing in the final match of the 1981/82 season to Sheffield Wednesday 2-1 at Hillsborough, City were promoted back to the First Division at the first attempt after relegation. City managers of the future, Martin O'Neill and John Deehan, celebrate Bertschin's goal, whilst Dave Watson gives a clenched-fist salute. Ken Brown's side had finished third behind Luton Town and Watford.

Plans for The new River End stand and the building bond scheme starting in August 1981.

A photograph showing the devastation of the old main stand, which caused City problems during the early months of the 1984/85 season. Just two days after the fire, City were at home to Queens Park Rangers, and in this picture manager Ken Brown takes a look at the charred remains of the structure.

In October 1984 the main stand at Carrow Road was ruined by fire. This photograph shows leading fire-fighter Dave Case picking out trophies from the charred remains; City lost many cups and souvenirs in the blaze. Ironically, the club would win the Milk Cup later that season, which was, however, dogged by further disappointment. City lost their First Division place yet again and, although qualifying for European football for the first time in their history, they were then to find themselves banned with all other English clubs due to the tragic events at the Heysel Stadium at the end of that season.

Saturday 1 October 1983 saw the visit of Manchester United to Carrow Road. Two goals by Norman Whiteside and one from Frank Stapleton had given the Reds a comfortable 3-0 lead, but an amazing second-half comeback through goals by Dave Bennett and Mike Channon was finally rounded off with a last-minute equaliser by Louie Donowa to give City an incredible 3-3 draw. In this picture, Louie Donowa (leaning back), hits the last goal of the game, with Mike Channon also in attendance.

Ken Brown's side won the Milk Cup semi-final over rivals Ipswich Town, despite having lost the first leg on 23 February 1985 at Portman Road 1-0 to an early Mich D'Avray goal. The second leg on 6 March caused great jubilation for Norwich fans at Carrow Road after John Deehan had equalised in the 35th minute, and Steve Bruce headed home the winner with just three minutes remaining. City had won 2-1 on aggregate to reach Wembley for the third time.

The Milk Cup final team of 1985. It was a case of third time lucky at Wembley as the Canaries were 1-0 winners over Sunderland. Asa Hartford, who was making history as the first player to appear at Wembley in three League Cup finals for different clubs, fittingly scored the 46th minute winner with a deflected shot off Sunderland's Gordon Chisholm. Amazingly, City's Dennis Van Wyk then handled in the penalty area barely a minute later, but was relieved to see Clive Walker's effort clip the post (making him the first player to miss a penalty in a Wembley final). The team was, from left to right, back row: Mel Machin (chief coach), Louie Donowa, Steve Bruce, Chris Woods, Dave Watson (captain), John Deehan, John Devine (substitute). Front row: Mark Barham, Peter Mendham, Paul Haylock, Mike Channon, Dennis Van Wyk, Asa Hartford.

The team arriving at City Hall with the Milk Cup.

Milk Cup final programme.

Mike Channon in a familiar pose. Mike made his City debut on 27 December 1982 in a First Division match at Portman Road, City winning 3-2. He made 108 appearances for Norwich, including the 1985 Milk Cup final, and scored 25 goals. Mike left City for Portsmouth at the beginning of the 1985/86 season. City were to win back their First Division place for the third time at the first attempt in this season, following promotion in 1974/75 and 1981/82. This time though, they were Second Division champions and Ken Brown's side were back in the top flight in some style!

14 February 1987 and Her Royal Highness The Duchess of Kent opens the new City stand and meets the City team. Here, she is photographed shaking hands with top marksman Kevin Drinkell. City were now back in the First Division and even finished in the top five – their highest ever League position at the time. The subsequent match versus Manchester City ended in a 1-1 draw, with Ian Crook gaining a point for City.

Manager Dave Stringer took his side to fourth in the First Division in 1988/89 and the furthest in the FA Cup since that day in 1959, although it was more semi-final heartbreak with a 1-0 defeat at Villa Park against Everton. The disappointment was put in perspective by tragic events in the other semi-final at Hillsborough. In this picture, Malcolm Allen celebrates one of his two goals past 'keeper Phil Parkes, which helped put West Ham out of the quarter-finals with a 3-1 win in the replay at Carrow Road.

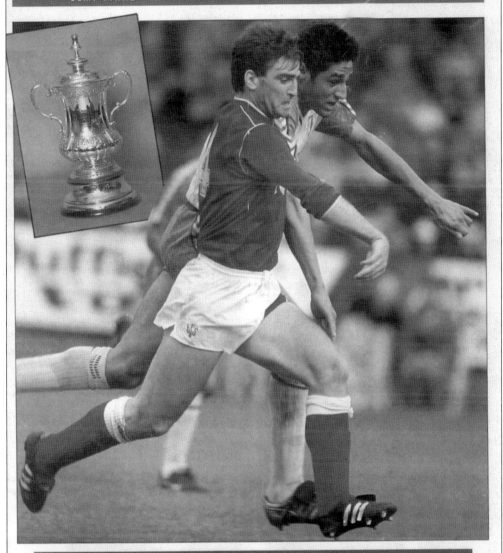

THE F.A. CHALLENGE CUP

SEMI-FINAL ◆ AT VILLA PARK ◆ SATURDAY 15TH APRIL 1989

EVERTON v NORWICH CITY

OFFICIAL MATCH MAGAZINE ◆ PRICE ONE POUND

One step from Wembley on 15 April 1989 and – after defeating Port Vale, Sutton United, Sheffield United and West Ham – City reached the semi-finals to face Everton.

Robert Rosario, Trevor Putney, Ian Crook and Bryan Gunn walk off the field after the 1989 semi-final defeat against Everton.

Robert Fleck joined City from Glasgow Rangers in December 1987 for £580,000, making his debut two days later at Wimbledon on 18 December. Robert made 166 appearances for Norwich and became the club's top scorer for four seasons in a row, with a total of 66 goals, before leaving the club in a £2.1 million move to Chelsea at the start of the 1992/93 season. He returned to the club in 1995 for £750,000 and made his second debut on 30 August 1995 at home against Oldham, making a further 105 appearances with another 18 goals before leaving at the end of the 1997/98 season. His total of 84 goals makes him the third highest scorer in the club's history.

Six

Europe, Relegation and Beyond

City gained their highest League position in 1992/93, the first season of the FA Premiership. In Mike Walker's first season in charge, City finished third and qualified for Europe. In fact, City led the table with just six matches to go, before losing 3-1 at home to the eventual Champions Manchester United. This picture shows Munich hero Jeremy Goss with manager Mike Walker after a 1-1 draw at Carrow Road, in which he had scored in yet again.

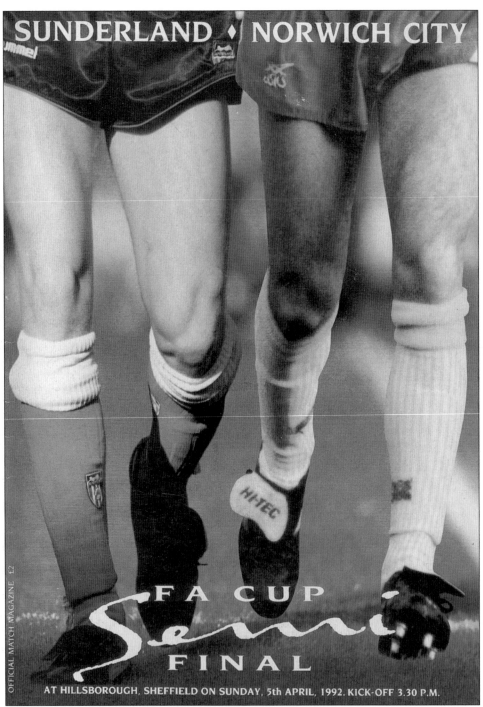

SUNDERLAND ◆ NORWICH CITY

FA CUP Semi FINAL

AT HILLSBOROUGH, SHEFFIELD ON SUNDAY, 5th APRIL, 1992. KICK-OFF 3.30 P.M.

OFFICIAL MATCH MAGAZINE £2

Norwich City really fancied their chances of making it third time lucky and reaching Wembley for the first time in the FA Cup in 1992, but as in 1959 and 1989, it was a single goal defeat which halted the dream yet again for Dave Stringer's side. Second Division Sunderland took the field at Wembley instead and Norwich had now missed out for the second time in playing Liverpool at Wembley in the FA Cup final.

118

Mark Robins joined the club from Manchester United and made an explosive debut for Norwich against Arsenal at Highbury on 15 August 1992 – City's first season of FA Premiership football. The first game of the 1992/93 season ended 4-2 to City with Robins scoring two of them after coming on as substitute – giving the City fans much hope for the season ahead following the disappointment of the sale of the popular Robert Fleck to Chelsea just before the start of the campaign. Mark made 64 appearances for City, scoring 21 goals.

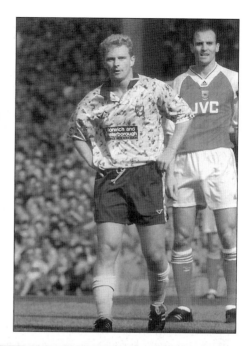

Chris Sutton, son of former player and coach Mike, made his debut for the Norwich City youth side in April 1989, going on to the first team for his debut on 4 May 1991. He made a total of 113 appearances for the Canaries, scoring 43 goals. He was sensationally sold in July 1994 before the start of the 1994/95 season to Blackburn Rovers for £5 million, when chairman Robert Chase had repeatedly stated 'If Chris Sutton is not here at the start of next season, neither will I be.' Sutton went and Chase stayed. In this photograph, Chris Sutton beats Swindon's Adrian Whitbread in a goalless draw at Carrow Road on 28 August 1993.

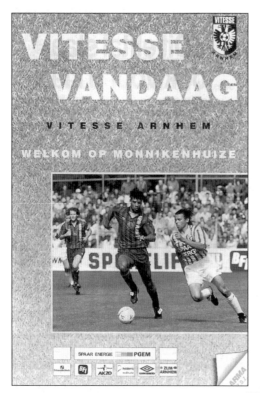

City's European adventure started with a 3-0 home win over Dutch side Vitesse Arnhem in the first leg at Carrow Road. Efan Ekoku scored City's first goal in European competition after 50 minutes. Further goals were added by Jeremy Goss and captain John Polston. The return brought a goalless draw and a satisfactory start to the UEFA Cup as far as City supporters were concerned.

Few supporters would have believed that City would face the famous German side Bayern Munich at Carrow Road in the second leg just needing a draw to go through to the third round, but thanks to glorious strikes by Jeremy Goss and Mark Bowen that was just the scenario. The second leg on 3 November 1993 attracted a crowd of 20,829 and, despite Adolfo Valencia giving the Germans an equaliser after just 5 minutes, it was that man Jeremy Goss with a 50th minute strike that gave City a 3-2 aggregate victory.

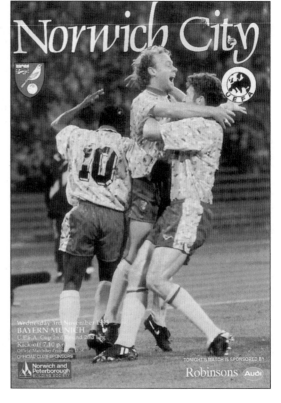

The Bayern Munich programme for the first leg against Norwich City.

Evening News

LATE FINAL

UEFA Cup Souvenir Special

Norwich, Wednesday, October 20, 1993

26p

Our true British grit — Walker

EURO-HEROES!

City's victory restores English pride

VERDICT: *back page*

REPORT: *page 30-31*

CHEERS! City manager Mike Walker and goal hero Jeremy Goss celebrate the Canary victory over Bayern Munich at the Olympic Stadium. Walker told the Evening News: "We showed true British grit to pull off this result. You can achieve anything if you really want to do it. If you go out to be negative, you don't win things."

■ Home leg ticket queues — page 3
■ Opinion — page 8

PHOTO: SIMON FINLAY

MAGNIFICENT Norwich City were basking in Euro-glory today after restoring the pride of English football with the greatest night in the club's history.

The Canaries' stunning 2-1 UEFA Cup victory in Munich's Olympic Stadium last night put them well on the way to waving "bye-bye, Bayern" — and could open the door to a whopping £5 million haul for the club.

The first-leg win over the German giants should ensure Norwich's place in the third round of the competition.

City chairman Robert Chase said: "We have already made

Reports by Jonathan Ilott, Beth Rose, and Tim Miller

£1 million, and the contract with the BBC is now worth an extra £50,000. If we go all the way in this competition, I'm told we can make £5 million.

He predicted that the extra cash now brought the new South Stand redevelopment closer to reality.

But Mr Chase warned: "We have still got to finish Bayern off in a fortnight's time."

Munich's own morning paper said that the Canaries had plucked Bayern and their team now needed a miracle for the return leg.

At Carrow Road this morning, dozens of eager fans were queuing outside the box office before it opened to ensure they got tickets for the second leg on November 3.

There were about 2000-2500 tickets left at noon today, but manager Roger King predicted a 20,600 sell-out within days.

Mr Chase also revealed today that the club would be trying to get the go-ahead to instal an extra 600-plus seats in the unfinished Barclay corner stand in time for the return match.

Norwich City supporters also helped to restore the tarnished reputation overseas of English football fans. German police

praised the behaviour of City's 1200-strong army, reporting only four arrests.

Two people were arrested in Munich before the game and two after the match.

Before the game, bookies quoted Norwich at 11-2 to beat Bayern and 40-1 to win the cup. "Those odds will come down a bit now," said a spokesman for John Slapp bookmakers in Norwich.

● Nobody could say that Canaries fans were not On The Ball before last night's match. The favourite result on the Evening News hotline to predict the score was 2-1 to Norwich!

GIVE US A CALL!   ■ NEWSDESK: NORWICH 628311   ■ ADVERTISING: NORWICH 660101

The Evening News headline on 20 October 1993, after City had just won in the Olympiastadion – becoming the first British team to beat the Bayern side in Europe on their own ground.

Jeremy Goss with his 20-yard volley in Munich ... 1-0!

Ian Butterworth powers his header goalwards in the Bayern Munich penalty-area during the game at the Olympiastadion.

Ruel Fox in action in the Sans Siro in the third round against Inter Milan. City lost both legs 1-0, but Mike Walker's side had enjoyed a memorable European experience. Unfortunately, things were about to go horribly wrong for the club.

Norwich City

Wednesday 24th November 1993
F.C. INTERNAZIONALE
UEFA Cup 3rd Round 1st Leg
Kick-off 7.10 p.m.
Official Matchday Programme £1.50
OFFICIAL CLUB SPONSORS

Norwich and
Peterborough
BUILDING SOCIETY

TONIGHT'S MATCH IS SPONSORED BY

Royal Mail

ANGLIA

The programme for the first leg with FC Internazionale.

Evening News

LATE FINAL

Norwich, Thursday, December 9, 1993   26p

Coming tomorrow don't miss
extra
Your new 16-page guide

CAN'T WIN 'EM ALL!

Some you win, some you lose! Joy Goss, mum of City midfield star Jeremy Goss, takes a philosophical view of the Canaries UEFA Cup exit.   PHOTO: SIMON FINLAY

No more money – Chase

CANARIES' chairman Robert Chase has rejected calls from manager Mike Walker for more cash for the players.

Chase, speaking after the team's heroics against Inter Milan, warned that the club is not going to "kick ourselves into a spiralling wage circle."

■ No changes — back page

Norwich City may have lost the war but won the battle, according to the national Press today.

● Daily Mail: "Norwich have the gratitude of English football for demonstrating that the so-called poorer relations can not only survive against the might of Italy but outplay them, too."

● Today: "Mike Walker wiped away tears of injustice and pride as Norwich City's European crusade came to a noble end."

● Mirror: "The dream is over — and the tears flowed after Norwich went out of Europe but earned the glory."

● The Independent: "Norwich reminded the rest of Europe that English footballers can still play the game the way it was meant to be played."

CITY may have lost the tie but they've won friends all over Europe.

Mike Walker's men can hold their heads high. They gave us all some magic memories that will stay with us for the rest of our lives. New generations will have to get used to hearing about the glory days back in '93.

And they were glory days indeed. To celebrate we'll be staging a special reception for the team to recognise their achievement. Some fans will have a chance to take part and we'll give you details soon.

The Canaries looked the part as they strutted on to the European stage blowing away mighty Bayern Munich and giving Inter Milan a fight they never expected in the overpowering atmosphere of the mighty San Siro stadium.

City left us with magic memories

Defeated they may be but the Canaries were simply superb. All the national pundits, yes even including BBC's less-than-generous Alan Hansen, became fans of the Canary style.

With the English national team at its lowest ebb, City showed that English football can compete with the best.

The principles of open, passing football that are now part of the Norwich style have established the Canaries in the top flight of English football and

OPINION by the editor

won friends all over Europe. They really were that good.

Lifelong City supporter Derek Bill, of Thorpe End, summed it up for many fans. "This has been the best day of my life — really tremendous," he said.

"We didn't deserve to lose but it just wasn't to be."

The team's achievements were matched by the fans. As chair-

man Robert Chase said: "The supporters were a credit to the club and to the country. It did a power of good for English football."

Manager Mike Walker agreed: "The fans were unbelievable. After the game they just stayed on and on. It's something I'll never forget."

And Mike and his boys gave us performances that we'll never forget. It's been great. We're proud of them.

■ Fans fly home — page 3

GIVE US A CALL!   ■ NEWSDESK: NORWICH 628311   ■ ADVERTISING: NORWICH 660101

The Evening News report on the defeat in Milan and the writing is already on the wall.

Happier days in the Premiership as City supporters enjoy some flag waving for the *Match of the Day* cameras during a staged screening in August 1993. By the beginning of 1994, Mike Walker, who had asked for more cash for players, had resigned and joined Everton – barely a month after the European dream had came to an end. John Deehan took the managerial chair. Players were also on their way, with Chris Sutton being sold. By the end of the 1994/95 season, City lost their place in the Premiership, with Gary Megson in the unenviable position of taking the Canaries down having adopted a caretaker role near the end of the season. City were now back in the old Second Division, Division One, but their drop did not prompt an immediate return as on the previous three occasions. Old boy Martin O'Neill had been brought in by Robert Chase as manager, but he resigned before Christmas, leaving Gary Megson to step in again. The Canaries finished the season a disappointing sixteenth position in the table. Chairman Robert Chase then sold his shares to Geoffrey Watling, prompting scenes of celebration on the terraces during City's last match at Crystal Palace. In 1996/97, Mike Walker returned to the manager's position. However, City nearly dropped into Division Two in 1997/98 and new managers arrived in quick succession – Bruce Rioch for the 1998/99 season, followed by Bryan Hamilton in March 2000 and then Nigel Worthington, who took charge during the 2000/01 season. Norwich City end their first century of football outside the top flight, but are hopeful that they will get back to where the majority of supporters now expect the club to be. Just think that 100 years ago the club were playing in the Norfolk & Suffolk League!

Andy Marshall made his City debut on 27 December 1994, during City's last season of Premiership football. He came on as a substitute at Nottingham Forest, replacing the injured Bryan Gunn, and then played for the rest of the season, missing just three games to Simon Tracey. For the next two seasons he only got his chance in a handful of matches, but finally got his chance of becoming the first-choice 'keeper from the 1997/98 season. He made a total of 222 appearances for Norwich. A former England under-21 international, Andy is regarded as one of the best young 'keepers in the country and won the Player of the Year award in 2000/01. The speculation regarding his future at Norwich, however, was answered just before the beginning of the 2001/02 season when he joined Ipswich Town on a free transfer to replace his close friend, Richard Wright. Marshall thus became the first Norwich player to move to Ipswich for fifteen years, John Deehan being the last way back in 1986.

Just before Andy Marshall's departure, Norwich signed Mark Rivers from Crewe Alexandra for £600,000. It was the most City had paid out since Iwan Roberts joined from Wolves in 1997 for £850,000. Rivers is one of several new players to join Norwich for the beginning of the 2001/02 season.